ZERO TO BREAKTHROUGH

The 7-Step, Battle-Tested Method for Accomplishing Goals That Matter

VERNICE *"FlyGirl"* ARMOUR

GOTHAM
BOOKS

GOTHAM BOOKS
Published by Penguin Group (USA) Inc.
375 Hudson Street, New York, New York 10014, U.S.A.
Penguin Group (Canada), 90 Eglinton Avenue East, Suite 700, Toronto, Ontario M4P 2Y3, Canada
(a division of Pearson Penguin Canada Inc.) • Penguin Books Ltd, 80 Strand, London WC2R
0RL, England • Penguin Ireland, 25 St Stephen's Green, Dublin 2, Ireland (a division of Penguin
Books Ltd) • Penguin Group (Australia), 250 Camberwell Road, Camberwell, Victoria
3124, Australia (a division of Pearson Australia Group Pty Ltd) • Penguin Books India Pvt Ltd,
11 Community Centre, Panchsheel Park, New Delhi—110 017, India • Penguin Group (NZ),
67 Apollo Drive, Rosedale, North Shore 0632, New Zealand (a division of Pearson New Zealand
Ltd) • Penguin Books (South Africa) (Pty) Ltd, 24 Sturdee Avenue, Rosebank, Johannesburg
2196, South Africa

Penguin Books Ltd, Registered Offices: 80 Strand, London WC2R 0RL, England

Published by Gotham Books, a member of Penguin Group (USA) Inc.

First printing, April 2011
10 9 8

LIBRARY OF CONGRESS CATALOGING-IN-PUBLICATION DATA
has been applied for

ISBN 978-1-592-40624-1

Printed in the United States of America
Set in Minion Pro
Designed by Elke Sigal

While the author has made every effort to provide accurate telephone numbers and Internet
addresses at the time of publication, neither the publisher nor the author assumes any responsibility for errors, or for changes that occur after publication. Further, the publisher does not have
any control over and does not assume any responsibility for author or third-party Web sites or
their content.

ZERO TO BREAKTHROUGH

To Mom and Dad . . . and Mom and Dad.
You told me I could do anything.

To my twin flame . . .
we're going to do so much more!

CONTENTS

FOREWORD

by Mae Jemison, MD

Everyone has and strives for moments when their passions, training, and talents "click"—match the circumstances and create success.

Whether providing armed tactical air support in a Cobra helicopter to hemmed-in ground troops in Iraq, responding as a police officer to a burglary call, competing in a bodybuilding contest, or giving a speech to hundreds of people—success, in each situation, required Captain Vernice Armour (Ret. USMC) to have mastered specific capabilities. In *Zero to Breakthrough*, Captain Armour, through examples from her own remarkable life and those of others, tells us—in succinct, straightforward, U.S. Marine fashion—her strategies for making and exceeding her ambitions for her life and how you can, too.

Brief history: I met Vee—as I like to call her—during a project organized by my foundation called Celebrating Women of Color in Flight. As a former NASA astronaut and the first woman of color in the world to go into space, I was thrilled to promote and highlight all these incredible women who came together from around the world to change the face of aviation and aerospace. And as the group got to know one another in between subcommittees and a packed schedule of school visits, flight festivals, galas, and public relations outreach, I was struck by how Vee stood out among the field of so many remarkable and outstanding women. Her enthusiasm was infectious. She was the consummate *"We can do this"* (emphasis on the "we") colleague and team member. Her sense of humor helped clear difficult moments and put them in perspective. And her talks riveted audiences. Plus, she was cool and competent. The kind of person you trust when she says "I've got your six" (or "I've got your back" in civilian talk). I'm proud to call her a friend and colleague.

Which brings me to Zero to Breakthrough (Z2B). More than three years ago, Vee asked me if I would write the foreword to her book. She didn't know exactly what the book would be, but she knew she was going write one. "Sure," I said, thinking, "She'll forget. It's a long way off, and she doesn't even have the book substance yet." But she did have the focus, planning, execution skills, and commitment to accomplish her ambition. And that's what Z2B is about. Identifying, prioritizing, and accomplishing ambitions that are important to you. So, here I am.

In Z2B Vee shares how she identifies, analyzes, and digests personal experiences and ambitions as a Marine, police officer, and athlete. She tells about how the Marines helped her to develop mental toughness and determination, but I know that she must have had some before the Marines, or she would never have gotten there. Yes, Vee was a woman combat pilot in the U.S. Marines, a motorcycle cop, and a public speaker, and obviously had a lot to work with—so do we all. She just learned to exploit hers—and now she shares with us how. Vee describes how to plan, stop procrastinating, distinguish between obstacles you can control and those you cannot, and execute and benefit from lessons learned and quiet time. Men and women whose ambitions are outsized, larger than life, far-flung adventures, or those who stay closer to the hearth, will find great insight. Z2B is helpful for various aspects of leading a fulfilling life by providing insights subtle and obvious, but all necessary for success—however you come to define it. Vee puts into clear language things we inherently know but fail to act on because they are lost in the back of our minds somewhere.

So, here is the bottom line: I like to think I am no slouch when it comes to taking on challenges and achieving my goals. But we can all use some extra motivation from time to time. Reading Vee's manuscript in preparation to write the foreword has given me a kick of "umph" to fully engage in several upcoming projects, drop others, and maybe even dust off and keep a New Year's resolution.

Enjoy.
Mae Jemison, MD

Dr. Mae Jemison's remarkable career as a doctor, engineer, scientist, academic, entrepreneur, and public intellectual includes six years with NASA as a space shuttle astronaut making history as the first woman of color in the world to go into space. Jemison practiced medicine in Sierra Leone, West Africa; was a professor of environmental studies at Dartmouth College; and founded a nonprofit educational foundation specializing in science literacy and technology. A member of the National Academy of Sciences' Institute of Medicine, author and highly sought-after speaker, Dr. Jemison has garnered many of the nation's highest national, academic, and institutional honors for her work. And she was the first person to appear on an episode of *Star Trek* who had actually ever been in space.

INTRODUCTION

Straight Up and Straight Ahead

If you do what average people do,
you'll have what average people have.
I don't want to be average. Do you?

—VERNICE "FLYGIRL" ARMOUR

A Breakthrough Mentality is refusing to settle even in the smallest of moments and demanding a breakthrough life. You already have the potential to be extraordinary—everyone does. The Marines have a philosophy: Leaders are made, not born. That's good news. It means our energy and passion can be harnessed through discipline and practice and channeled into dynamic, positive action and accomplishment. *Zero to Breakthrough* is a proven, surefire strategy to recognize your passion and purpose; create a game plan to make it real; and keep on track to getting there when life gets in the way. Seriously.

> *Breakthrough* is the ability to innovate and implement creative solutions using your passion, natural aptitudes, and interests to accomplish personal ambitions and fulfill your life purpose.

All of us have passions fueled by fire inside of us—those dreams and ideas that are itching to get out but we just don't know how to open the door to making them a reality. You need to reach breakthrough moments: innovate and implement creative solutions using passion, natural aptitudes, and interests to accomplish personal ambitions and fulfill your life purpose. *Zero to Breakthrough* is the flight plan to get you there. It includes original strategies such as passion identification and backward planning, learning when and how to reroute your journey to avoid obstacles, and mastering momentum to reach future victories.

I hold fast to the theory that there's no such thing as a dream out of reach. *Zero to Breakthrough* tells you how to accelerate from where you are and set out to get what you're itching to do, *done*—regardless of where you're starting out from and no matter where you've been. I also discuss preparation, strategy, courage, legacy (or how you plan to leave things when you're gone), and the importance of high spirits and enthusiasm. Taken together, these concepts create a sustainable inner force and conviction that results in meeting goals, accomplishing significant tasks, and becoming an extraordinary member of the community. And damn if you're not going to have fun trying, doing, and succeeding!

Zero to Breakthrough: The 7-Step, Battle-Tested Method for Accomplishing Goals That Matter answers the question I get asked most often from people who hear my story: "Vernice, how do you get big things done?" Okay, let me pause here and give you some background.

Before I was thirty I had the privilege of serving as the *first* black female—and only the second female—motorcycle policewoman in Nashville, Tennessee, and the *first* black female police officer for the Tempe, Arizona, Police Department. In December 1998, I beat a few odds and realized my dream of becoming a United States Marine Corps Officer. In July 2001, I became the Corps' *first* African-American female pilot. Then, in March 2003, I was recognized by the Department of Defense as the *first* African-American female combat pilot for flying the famed AH-1W Super Cobra helicopter during my two tours in Iraq.

After successfully completing two tours as a pilot during Operation Iraqi Freedom, I made the difficult decision to leave the military. In August 2007, I received a warm sendoff from the Marine Corps, and continued to fulfill my purpose—to protect and serve—in a different way. The military had confirmed my long-held belief that everyone has a unique gift or talent to share that no one else has. Everyone in the armed forces is tested, categorized, trained, and promoted according to what they are really good at. As a result, we can perform at our peak and excel for the optimum benefit of our comrades and the public we serve.

After I left the service, I noticed that that there are few people who are expert at crossing off objectives from their life lists—those files of "somedays" and "I'd love tos" that we all have tucked away in our heads. I'm not talking about checking things off of a to-do list (fix the garbage disposal, mow the lawn): Accomplishing significant goals and bringing to reality long-held aspirations is what concerns me.

For the last two years, I have been a motivational leadership speaker and have shared the Zero to Breakthrough method with hundreds of thousands of individuals (and I'm just warming up) at government agencies (including the Department of Defense and the U.S. Naval Academy), corporate entities (such as Raytheon, Bank of America, and Booz Allen Hamilton), technology firms (including Boeing and IBM), and associations (Women in Cable Telecommunications and the Professional and Scientific Association, to name two). During the informal meet and greet reception before my speeches, audience members typically tell me:

"We were so excited when we found out you were a pilot. Wow! But you're black and a woman. The Marines are pretty tough. Did you face any obstacles?"

Of course I've had to overcome my share of barriers, especially being a woman in many male-dominated fields. But obstacles never held me back or frightened me off unless I let them. Prevailing over impediments is within our control. I managed to keep running and rising, despite the adversity that I confronted or (sometimes mistakenly) perceived—keeping the vision and ultimate goal in mind with the support of great teamwork.

Everyone hits walls; walls exist to be taken down. Too often we allow what we think is an impenetrable roadblock to stop us, and we avoid our big dreams in favor of an easier route. That's where Zero to Breakthrough comes in. My seven Z2B steps will help you unearth, cultivate, and grow your talents and accelerate your passion (I call it *EXCEL*erated Passion).

I've heard some amazing results from people who have used Zero to Breakthrough. Take, for instance, the man who heard my talk at a veterans' organization. George had recently been let go from a long-time job and he was too close to retirement age to get another similarly high-powered corporate position. He rediscovered his *umph*—a zeal for woodworking—by identifying his passion. Investing in quiet time and doing my Z2B exercise Start Your Engines (described in Chapter 1) brought him back to the time he enjoyed as a young man working with his father on building projects.

George realized that without a full-time job, he had the time to lay the groundwork for his own success. Using Step Two of Zero to Breakthrough, Stop Procrastinating and Prepare, he learned about the latest tools and equipment for woodworking and the needs of his local community. From there a successful carpentry business was born. Today, he teaches young people building skills at a local youth center—and, in turn, hires the most talented to work in his now large and busy shop. That's the big breakthrough: carrying on a legacy and helping others achieve their own breakthrough moments by using your own passions and talents.

The manager at the Defense Supply Center in Richmond, Virginia, an organization that supports the military, told me of an employee, Diane, who was disruptive to her team. Diane implemented Zero to Breakthrough after hearing me speak; she used the program to take back personal responsibility for her job and implement more efficient system controls. By using and applying her knowledge of math and computers (a crucial part of Step One is to find your passion by using your God-given talents) to overcome internal and external roadblocks (a key goal of Step Four), Diane was able to troubleshoot problems while keeping her own best interests in mind, which helped both her and the operation succeed. Using Step Six, Success Is Not a Final Destination, Diane built on her initial achievement and was able to innovate more efficiencies on the delivery side of the business. Her manager said that "almost overnight" she became a positive force for her team—and for herself.

Environmental Protection Agency workers, including scientists and researchers, felt a renewed commitment to their roles through the legacy-building aspects of Zero to Breakthrough. My question to employees of large organizations like the EPA always is: Can you see what you do with fresh eyes? Do your on-the-job accomplishments and breakthroughs contribute to your satisfaction as an employee and a person as well as to the well-being of others?

What we do and how we do it is *that* important: It's the ripple effect. You may think that federal employees are fired up and fully aware that what they do is for the greater good. This is a misconception; there is tremendous burnout in the federal sector, caused by multilayered bureaucracy, and results are often unseen for months and sometimes years. Many individuals working in large institutions don't always see how their jobs make an actionable difference to the institution's mission, let alone our society.

Along with the level of happiness and incredible exhilaration that finding and following your passion provides, Zero to Breakthrough also inspires and encourages a strong desire to become a responsible and caring member of society. Why should you care? Why *wouldn't* you care, is my question. Leaving a lasting legacy through personal achievement means that you have made a difference. That's why I have made making a positive impact an underlying theme in *Zero to Breakthrough,* and also why I share my program at youth centers and organizations and with women in prison.

We all have an obligation to use the blessings, gifts, and talents we have with passion fueled by fire—what I refer to simply as *umph*—to leave a positive mark on the planet. Hey, we are already here, and we definitely are going to leave a mark. Don't you want yours to matter?

The Marine Corps' core philosophy explains it: Make a place better having been there than it was before you came. I hold faithful to that spirit and want to light the flame in others. My real agenda is to create—through lectures, this book, and social media—a Zero to Breakthrough *movement* of inspired courage and action. It may be the most important and daring challenge of my life.

Here, at a glance, are the seven strategies you'll learn to use in *Zero to Breakthrough:*

Step One: Develop Consciousness and Awareness

Identifying what your passions are is the best way to find your purpose in life. It is the only way to get on the launchpad. Goal: Recognize what you're good at and how you really want to be spending your time.

Step Two: Stop Procrastinating and Prepare

If you do what average people do, you'll have what average people have. No one reaches an objective by mistake. Goal: Unblock and release beliefs, fears, and past experiences that might be holding you down, and then lay the groundwork for success.

Step Three: Execute Situations with Self-Discipline

Assessing and responding to unexpected situations and executing and revising them in real time to get a desired result takes discipline and understanding. Goal: Practice consistency and continue to achieve mastery.

Step Four: Acknowledge and Move Past Obstacles and Challenges

Do you need to get through, around, under, or over the obstacle? Learn how to acknowledge obstacles without giving them power and letting them stop you. Goal: Learn how to overcome external and internal roadblocks and troubleshoot problems without doing damage to your own best interests.

Step Five: Feel Fear and Focus Anyway

Learn how to feel the fear and use it to keep charging. Goal: Understand that fear is real, but it does not have to derail you.

Step Six: Success Is Not a Final Destination

Once we have accomplished a mission, we have to keep the momentum going. Honor the past and see into the future without dwelling on either one. Understand your strategic advantages to expand your horizons. Goal: Use one accomplishment or success to build toward others.

Step Seven: Complete Integration

Breakthrough goes beyond one accomplishment; it's bigger than reaching a destination and continuing the flight. It is a complete integration of Zero to Breakthrough into daily life, and living like a leader. It's also about leaving a legacy. Goal: Make Z2B a natural part of your everyday approach to life—to become a leader, engage new ideas, live life fully, and be a model for your children, community, employees, and employers.

HOW TO USE THE BOOK

Zero to Breakthrough can be read from start to finish. It's succinct and focused (hey, I'm a Marine!), but I've also tried to make it as interactive as possible, by including case studies and exercises (*do* try them at home). In fact, it's a good idea to read it once straight through and then go back to the sections that resonate with you the most, or reread the areas that you feel you need the most help or encouragement with.

One point about the case studies—they take a look at real-life situations in which people or companies were able to achieve a breakthrough. These sections have two take-aways, or fly-aways, as I call them. First, they are instructive and inspiring in and of themselves. But more than that, they demonstrate a way of reading business and personal achievement stories and breaking them down into their essential elements. The people who have walked the path before you offer lessons, and my case studies give you one way of understanding the elements of their stories that you can use. I urge you to look for case studies of your own, in books, business magazines, and newspapers and from successful people you meet (pick their brains if they are open to it!) . . . wherever you find them.

If you're a manager in a business or a group leader, Zero to Breakthrough promotes teamwork, and in career development workshops it helps you identify the individual strengths of your people and suggests ways of channeling those skills profitably. It also works to build intellectually well-balanced teams, unleash the full potential of diversity for a positive impact on your bottom line, and create a culture that values and respects everyone's contributions. The case studies make effective jumping-off points for problem-solving discussions and brainstorming sessions.

If you are using the book as an individual to grow your career or meet a personal goal, here's a good idea—find yourself a Breakthrough Buddy to work with through the book, someone you trust and who shares your values and believes in your goals (and vice versa). In my experience, a buddy makes it more likely you'll stick with the strategies and stay with your plans. The power of these seven strategies is enhanced when you share and use them with someone else.

Families can use the book to encourage good citizenship and excellence at school. Chapters make great "conversation starters" at the family dinner table—on a Monday night you might talk about finding your passion, and by Friday your kids could be talking about what they learned about theirs through research. Teenagers and young people poised to enter college or the military (and who may be leaving home for the first time) can use it for guidance when the inevitable first taste of freedom can tempt them away from studying. I've written the book in plain English, and any military lingo used is defined so everyone can understand what I'm talking about. Now, let's suit up and take flight.

ZERO TO BREAKTHROUGH

CHAPTER 1

You're Not Stuck, You're Just Not Moving: Consciousness and Awareness

Some people spend an entire lifetime
wondering if they made a difference in the world.
But the Marines don't have that problem.

—RONALD REAGAN, PRESIDENT OF THE UNITED STATES

It was the end of one of those days. I'd worked really hard and was totally beat, but it was a good thing because the day had been productive. It was more than ten years ago, and I was interning as a personal trainer at a gym in Columbus, Ohio. The weight room had been busy, and there were plenty of clients to help. My car sputtered into the driveway; it was on its last leg. Now that I was home, all I wanted to do was put my feet up and chill. I checked my postbox and was happy to see that a friend had forwarded me a big yellow envelope filled with mail from Tennessee, as she had been doing every few weeks for the past few months.

I put my bag down and flipped through the contents—flyers, postcards from friends and family, and a few bills. Then I noticed the official seal of the City of Nashville in the left-hand corner of one envelope. I had taken the Nashville Civil Servants Exam more than a year ago, in hopes of jumping through the first hoop of getting into the Police Academy. "Wow," I thought, shaking my head, "the wheels of progress sure turn slowly." I anxiously ripped it open and read the contents.

"Dear Ms. Armour, Congratulations," and "come in for the next phase of testing" popped out at me. My heart sank when another phrase jumped off the page: "The next test is March 13 . . ." It was March 22. I had missed my chance! My dream since childhood was to become a cop, and it had just slipped through my fingers, not forever but at least for another year. How much time would go by before the next opportunity?

Not much, as it turned out. I quickly glanced at what was left of the stack and noticed a second letter with the distinctive blue and gold seal. "Since you were unable to attend the March 13 test, you can take the March 23 test . . ." I dropped the letter. *It was March 22.* Tomorrow. Okay. I'm exhausted. It's six o'clock. I haven't eaten dinner. My old clunker won't make the six-hour trip. I have about five hundred dollars in the bank—and five dollars in my pocket. I had clients to take care of at the gym the next day. No problem! I was *very* aware of what I had to do next.

I picked up the phone and called a friend. "Nadine, I need to borrow your car for a couple of days." After a few minutes of begging—I was not letting her off the line until she agreed to give me the keys to what was my future—she said yes. Early the next morning I made the drive to Nashville, arrived on time for the afternoon test, took it, and not that long after (this time it didn't take a year to get my results) found out I was eligible to enter the Academy. I did—and within two years I was the first African-American woman to be a Nashville motorcycle officer. Zero to Breakthrough.

The effort it took to get to Nashville wasn't a big deal. Whatever I had to do, whatever it cost me was worth it, because my burning desire to become a cop trumped everything else at that time. I knew it was a great training ground for my ultimate purpose in life: to help people.

Is there anything you think about that often, that you would make an at-any-cost effort for? Would you make the kind of leap I made to get to Nashville for the job you're doing now? The yes or no answer to that question tells you whether you are living your passion with *umph*—drive and enthusiasm.

If you answered yes, congratulations. You aren't stuck—you're moving! If you said no, then this chapter is for you. I'm going to help you become conscious and aware of exactly what your *umph* is. As you may already know, each one of us has something to offer—and it's usually found in what we truly love doing. In fact, no one else before you or after you has what you have in terms of talent and perspective. If you're not feeling your *umph,* you're probably not using your gifts to their fullest potential.

Combat Confidence: You're *good!* No one will be better at being you than *you.* Just the fact you are *the* authority on who you are, what you enjoy, and what you're good at should give you the courage to go after your passion with *umph.*

PASSION AND DRIVE EQUALS ACCOMPLISHMENT

What would happen if you started thinking of yourself, right now, as a person of great accomplishment? What might that mean about how you live your life and what you would be doing with your time? I'm going to take a guess and suggest that many of you would say that you'd be doing something very different from what you're doing now. You would rightly think that if you followed through on those changes you'd be living your life in a better, more enjoyable, and fully engaged way.

I have tremendous news: You *are* a person of great accomplishment, or at least you have the potential to be one. It's a matter of getting in touch with the stuff that is deep inside you, always itching to get out, that propels you forward and keeps you going even when you have no energy. I describe this phenomenon as *passion fueled by fire.* Passions are blessings, and that's why they aren't for us to keep to ourselves or abandon. We need to—we must—identify, develop, and share what we love. If we don't, going from Zero to Breakthrough will be an uphill battle.

The talents we possess offer us tremendous potential to be better—*the best*—at what we do, if we are willing to take possession of them. That potential, a solid asset, is our strategic advantage in life and business. Who doesn't want a leading edge? Yet talent is not exclusively about serving our own interests; it takes us beyond simply existing. A gift is both something you *receive* and something you *give*. In short, your passions are your purpose. The reason you are pulled in certain directions is bigger than yourself!

Everyone has at least one passion in life, if not more. Finding your passion is the first step in making an impact—going from Zero to Breakthrough. In my case, I want to help, serve, and protect others, but I'm also very passionate about sports and music. It's not by chance but by *design* that I was able to excel in law enforcement, the military, and sports. I had gifts related to those professions: social skills, the ability to think and act strategically, physical strength and agility, and technical aptitude. What do you know that you're good at?

Instead of beating my head against the wall by trying to fit into someone else's box doing something I didn't like because it seemed like the right thing to do, I chose paths that suited my talents, interests, and personality. It is the best way to start using the Zero to Breakthrough method.

When I was in college, I picked up a summer job working on a factory assembly line. Even temporary jobs can be educational—this one was typical assembly-line work, but the central goal involved pressing a button at specific time intervals.

My supervisor didn't think I did it very well, and she was right. I realized that while she was an expert at pressing that button at the right time, and that was cool, I didn't want to be there long enough to get good at it. Not only did I lack the button-pressing "gene," I had no interest in developing it. I didn't stay in that job long, and found another that suited my interests better (selling cell phones and plans, but that's a story for another time). Pressing that button just wasn't my passion.

Unfortunately, the noise and chatter and distractions of everyday life can cause some of us to keep pushing the wrong buttons in life. Our purpose gets lost or muted, shelved "for the time being," or worst of all, forgotten. At that point we give up even trying to rekindle the flame of passion we might have felt at one time—we can't even find the matches. When we try contemplating our burning desires, many of us freeze just like the proverbial deer in the headlights. What now? we ask. The worst cases may look back on their lives with great regret and sorrow. I'm not going to let any of that—least of all, inaction—happen.

READY FOR TAKEOFF?

Every once in a while I remind myself to have patience with people I talk to about connecting to their *umph* because I forget that it's not as easy for everyone as it was for me. My passion and *umph* happened in an instant when I was very young. My parents and I were in downtown Chicago when I was four years old. We were shopping on State Street, and I saw the mounted patrol for the first time. I had no idea that police officers rode horses. Those animals were glorious: I could see the strength of their muscles rippling under their shiny coats. My body vibrated with energy and excitement. That night sleep never really came— I just couldn't stop thinking about the larger-than-life officers enthroned on the backs of those incredible creatures.

I begged my parents to take me downtown every weekend; seeing the horses reinforced my desire to become one of the people who rode them. It was my own pint-size version of research and development. From the instant I saw the mounted police, I would not stop badgering my parents for a horse of my very own.

Flash-forward a couple of years. After my parents divorced, I found myself in a whole new world. My mom and her new husband, my brothers, and I recently had moved to California. It was Christmas morning. After opening all of our packages, Clarence, my stepfather (but always "Dad" to me), said to my brother and me, "Chris, Vernice, look outside the window." We ran to look at the backyard. There was the garden, the pool, and the barn. Check. Check. Check. Everything looked as it always did. "Come on, Vernice, look a little closer, look at the barn," Dad urged.

I focused hard on the barn, and then I saw it—*him*. My eyes got very big and I ran out the back door as fast as I could. There was a little colt poking his head out of one of the stalls. He was six months old, jet-black with a white star on his forehead. My dad had talked to our babysitter, Joann, who bred horses. Joann said we could have Midnight until it was time to break him in, so we were able to keep him for a year and a half.

His baby bones made him too fragile to ride, but he was still a horse! I learned a great deal about how to care for and groom horses with my Midnight. Still, I wanted to ride. After Midnight left to go back to the ranch with Joann, Clarence bought me Tera, a young pony that was big enough to ride. My dad saw how I was with Midnight and how I treated him, and he knew I'd be responsible with a bigger animal.

I entered into as many equestrian races and other competitions as I could, but Tera was only a pony and not as sizeable or powerful as my opponents' full-size horses. After one particular competition, we were walking home with a second-place ribbon in my hand. Amy and Apple (her horse) had beaten me again. I thought about the situation, and I said, "Daddy, Tera is running as fast as she can with her little legs; I need a big horse if I am going to win." At an early age, I learned the power of leverage (a bigger horse in this case) and having a strategic advantage (knowing how to ride well). Eventually, I managed to talk Clarence into getting a horse with longer legs. His name was Star, and when I was riding him, I felt like one, too.

I finally had the right horse—wasn't it only a matter of time before I became a cop? When I finish telling that story at keynote addresses and seminars, I often see eyes filled with desperation looking up at me—*how do I connect with my* umph *like Vernice did?* I can feel the audience's energy, eagerness, and anxiety—*how do I do it?* I look straight into their eyes and ask, "Is there something holding you back from digging a little deeper, from taking some action? What is keeping you from digging deeper, from taking that first step, no matter how small it may be?" Their thoughts and fears run along these lines:

"I can't."

"I'm way too busy trying to make ends meet."

"I might be too old now."

"I don't have a clue how to get started."

"I really don't even know what I'm passionate about anymore, I'm just so tired."

"No one would support me."

"Too hard."

To my mind, all these reasons add up to: *"I'm afraid to find out; I don't want to work for it; the risks are too great—what if I fail?"* We can stop the cycle of "maybe tomorrow," "totally impossible," and "I just can't" today—together. The payoffs of figuring out what you're most passionate about undoubtedly will outweigh any of the negatives you impose on yourself.

Combat Confidence: Find your Breakthrough Buddies (BTBs). There's a pad on the steps leading to the cockpit of a helicopter. You know, the nonskid gritty stuff that keeps you from slipping and falling. BTBs are your nonskid stuff. Who are the people who can support you so you don't fall when you're getting your *umph* on? Mom or Dad, friends, colleague, spouse or partner? The people who "watch your six" (if you are looking straight ahead, you are looking at twelve, and they look at six, behind you—watching your back) are your BTBs, your nonskid team. Gather them around from the beginning to help you focus on getting your *umph* on. *CAUTION: Beware of dream snatchers and energy vampires—you know, the people who leave you feeling totally drained.*

HELICOPTER STRATEGIES

People are more like helicopters and less like jets. We don't need a runway and we don't have to keep accelerating and moving at high speeds to reach our destination. We can lift ourselves right up from where we are. We can hover when necessary, recheck and reassess, and change altitude according to events. We can land where we want to, and go back up again from the same spot. What follows are six Zero to Breakthrough Helicopter Strategies that help develop consciousness, awareness, doability, and confirmation of your passion and purpose.

1. Take Off from Where You Are

No one is ever too old to be excited! I love being in touch with the kid inside of me, and I've worked really hard to stay that way. (There's a difference between acting childish and having childlike enthusiasm.) Have you ever watched kids in a playground? Notice how most get right up when they fall. They don't miss a beat—they just start over again, right from where they are: on the ground. That's how I want to be. I heard Les Brown say something very cool about this: "When you fall, make sure you land on your back. If you can see up, you can get up!"

Too often, when we "grow up" we shed our childlike wonder and our dreams become smaller and more contained. We tend to overthink matters instead of just starting in on them. There's a lot we can learn about young dreamers—they set no boundaries. For instance, not that long ago I met a very talkative seven-year-old boy named Asa. We shared the stage together at an event, and he was simply amazing. It was his first time speaking in front of a large audience, and he was a natural! On our ride back home, I sat in the back with him because I had to know more about how this little kid thought. By the time we got where we were going fifteen minutes down the road, he had not only told me his life story, but he shared his passion with me as well. I'll never forget when he looked at me and asked if I'd like to know how he found his purpose in life. I couldn't help but be immensely intrigued. He explained that it all happened at the age of four, when his mom took him to the zoo for the first time.

As soon as they entered the zoo, Asa and his mom headed straight for the reptile house. He ran up to the first habitat, and that's when he knew: Snakes would be his life. A few hours later he knew he wanted to become a herpetologist! Now, the first thought I had was "What the heck is a herpetologist?" Asa explained, with a laser-sharp intensity, that herpetologists work with snakes and other reptiles.

Now, I'm not sure how many of you have had a seven-year-old tell you they figured out their passion and purpose in life, but I was floored. And the zest he had for his passion was explosive! He didn't consider the pros and cons of pursuing a career in reptiles. He just went on to describe to me the different types of snakes and their habits. I decided to give him a little quiz. "If a snake tries to bite you but doesn't land his fangs into you, though the venom still comes out, how far does the venom stream spray?" He answered quickly, said approximately fifteen feet, and proceeded to tell me about the different types of venom. By the end of our conversation, I had no doubt that little Asa would be the best herpetologist who ever lived. And I knew more about snakes than I thought I'd ever need to know.

I recently read about an eleven-year-old who graduated from a Los Angeles college, and I was reminded again of Asa. When asked by a reporter what he wanted to do "when he grew up," the college grad (that's right, college grad), Moshe Kai Cavalin, rattled off a list that included studying astrophysics, mastering martial arts, writing a children's book, and learning to scuba dive.

I chuckled when I read this. Not because I thought, "Aren't youthful dreams adorable, and so unrealistic?" I smiled because young Moshe already has a Zero to Breakthrough mentality and is using it as the strategic advantage it truly is. "I feel it's a waste of time playing video games because it's not helping humanity in any way," the eleven-year-old said to explain the absence of kid stuff on his to-do list. He wants to use his knowledge to make the world a better place.

Now make your own childhood wish list—what were your ambitions at five, seven, or ten—fifteen or seventeen? Next, make a note of the things you wanted to do when you were in college. Write them down. If you have kids around, enlist their imaginations and help. What on your list have you actually done? Are you working in a field you were interested in as a youngster? Do you see a pattern emerging? For example, how many items on the list require similar skills (math, science, artistry) or a certain kind of environment (inside, outside, quiet, busy)?

Next, look at the immediate feasibility. If "rock star" is

on your list, can you dust off your instrument, practice, and sharpen your skills with a few music lessons—and then get a garage band together? It might be possible to book a few gigs around your town. You may in fact become a local guitar hero. Likewise, if you had an early interest in putting things together or building things, why not resurrect that hobby and start a side or full-time business making cabinets or repairing machines and electronics?

Keep in mind, though, that not all dreams can be fulfilled right away. I was watching a TV show that reported that Arnold Schwarzenegger's car detailer made more than $100,000 a year! You know he didn't start out making that kind of money. He probably started as a kid, washing his own cars and loving it. Then maybe he worked at the local car wash. Next he started a small business washing cars for others. At some point he was noticed as being one of the best detailers around. I'll be honest, I couldn't ever see myself washing cars for a living, performing heart surgery, or designing a skyscraper. But I do know this: Someone out there has a passion for those career paths, and their sheer *umph* for what they are doing will take them a million times further than the person who's just in it for some external reason—money, fame, or family pressure.

All you woodworkers and mechanically inclined out there, volunteer your know-how for Habitat for Humanity or a church group. You see where I'm going? There are powerful messages worth listening to in our long-ago childhood dreams, and living them is doable. These small steps can and do lead to big things—it's up to you to define whether *you* simply want to donate your expertise or use it to take your professional life in a whole different direction. We have so many resources around us that allow for our participation and growth, if we only stop and look for them.

2. You've Gotta Have Fun

What does fun have to do with taking off and flying like a helicopter? Because I'm sure you can only imagine how amazing and fun it is, riding up in the sky in a roller-coaster ride without wheels—so engaging that it's over before you even thought it began! Haven't you ever been so involved in a project that you lost complete track of time—when you looked at the clock, hours had passed? Anything we do that seamlessly demands and captures our attention should go on our passion list—even if it seems at first to be trivial or too "recreational."

Audience members and clients have told me their most engaging activities include tinkering with a car engine, baking a pie, playing an instrument, playing video games, practicing yoga, taking photos, and even bartending and creating unusual drinks for friends. One man told me he gets completely caught up with stargazing and identification—so much so that his wife often has to call him down from their roof deck at two in the morning.

What about on the weekends, when you're "playing"— what are the downtime activities that fill you with joy? What are your favorite chill pills—shopping with friends, cooking healthy and exotic food, watching movies in bed, or hanging with your dogs? (I, for one, love doing that.) These simple pleasures during "goofing-off time" offer additional indications of passion and purpose. I may volunteer in an animal shelter someday because I truly love my little furry friends.

I know of a woman who started a very successful business selling vintage garments, all as a result of expanding her love of beautiful clothes and shopping. I know of a "foodie" who, through networking, met a magazine editor who agreed to give her an assignment to write a story about whole grains. The story was so good that she got another assignment, and then another. Other magazines called, and now she writes regularly for three magazines. She volunteers at schools and soup kitchens, giving lessons and tips on eating well to children and adults making the transition from shelters to homes of their own.

Even nodding off in front of a flick can be expanded upon— I know of one guy whom many friends think of as lazy, but he has created his own movie review Web site and gets thousands of hits a week! The advertising dollars his site earns finance his life.

3. Keep Your Reserve Tank Full

Our current professions don't have to be our passion, and our passion does not have to be our profession. It would be awesome if that could always be the case, but it's not a requirement. Nevertheless, "day jobs" can be a central part of the system that enables us to experience and get closer to our passion and purpose. It's all a matter of attitude and reframing.

Besides, if you want to do something badly enough, a job will not stand in the way; it actually can help support your goals. Be grateful for employment, whether it's working the cash register at Walmart or bean counting for a financial firm. Think of it as your reserve tank, the fuel that keeps you going while you pursue greater things. When you leave for the day, you have the freedom and funds to work toward pursuing life as you really want to live it.

"I want to live my passion every day, Vernice," a young woman I'll call Keesha told me a few weeks ago. Keesha is in her mid-twenties and wants to fill as much of her time as possible working with young people. Feeling stuck in a job she doesn't care for, and dispirited about it, she asked me if she should quit. "Yes," I said, then added, "just not today, tomorrow, or next week." Instead of acting impulsively—and letting her reserve tank go empty—I suggested Keesha reframe her frustration and make that job (which had nothing to do with youth and everything to do with putting data into a computer) part of the *path* to her passion.

"Start looking at your job as the journey to fulfilling your dream, and not as drudgery that keeps you in a holding pattern," I said. After all, for a twenty-five-year-old not that long out of college, Keesha made a decent salary, enabling her to buy a house, pay her bills, save money, and, of course, have some fun. Plus, the fact that she was gaining real administrative and managerial capabilities would help her in any career. She liked being organized, and that was an asset to this job. Moreover, the job did not demand fifty or sixty or more hours per week. It was a straight nine-to-five gig. That left her plenty of time to volunteer at youth organizations, network with people who might steer her in the perfect direction, and research and plan her next move.

She was skeptical, of course, but the next day she promised to tell herself in the morning on her way to work, "I am blessed to have a job that I am good at and that fuels my plans for the future." Once the day started, Keesha found ways to be more efficient so she could use breaks to take mind-clearing walks, eat a nutritious lunch or snack, and do Internet research. Tasks she once thought of as boring now filled her with enthusiasm. "The faster and better I was able to get paperwork and chores off my desk, the more time I had for other things," she told me the next week. She also started to recognize that many things she had learned how to do on this job were actually preparing her for the youth foundation she was excited about starting. Her new breakthrough mentality was revealing all the tools and possibilities she had in her ammo for this current challenge on the battlefield.

Keesha successfully shifted her entire attitude and continued at the job. She learned administrative skills that would come in handy in foundation work, saved money, and had anxiety-free time to research and make contacts. She took her volunteer job at church to the next level and was able to recognize that although it was tough to split time between work and volunteering, it was giving her real-world experience and education that would take her from Zero to Breakthrough when she decided to start her foundation.

Are you, like Keesha, in a job that has no obvious relation to your passion? Don't walk away—especially if you need the steady paycheck. See it for what it can be: a way to finance your purpose. Can you cut back on your hours to make time for other career or entrepreneurial pursuits? Is it possible to speak to your manager about shifting your responsibilities to something you would enjoy or benefit more from? Or, if it is a job that is fairly repetitive and predictable, can you create an emotional distance from it and still do it well?

What do I mean by this? Remember *The Karate Kid* and "wax on, wax off"? In the movie, Daniel asks Mr. Miyagi to teach him karate but gets fed up with waxing his car and painting his fence, which feel like a waste of time. He's stunned to learn that the arm movements for these mundane tasks actually mirror martial arts blocks. Bottom line, I truly believe there is a lesson in everything we do. Take a step back and open yourself to the discovery of why you are here. Why are you in this job, and how is it taking you to the next level? Sometimes life doesn't take us to the next level until we have learned a certain lesson. Are you stalling yourself out and frustrating your dreams instead of seeing what you're doing as part of a process?

4. Safety Manuals Are Written in Stone

Safety manuals are essential when you're embarking on brand-new endeavors. Every do and don't in an aviation safety manual is there for a reason—to keep you safe and get you back to home base safely. That's the definition of a successful mission (safety-wise, anyway). When you're developing awareness around your passion, you need living, breathing safety manuals, or "safety people," who can help you stay on track through deed and example.

A while back, I had the great privilege of speaking to a group of young women incarcerated at the Cook County Jail in Chicago, Illinois. These women were in trouble, but social workers and guards at the prison saw something in them—a light that signaled they could turn themselves around. I often would see people like them when I was a correctional officer. A CO can tell the difference between a lifer (a career criminal) and a person who made a string of bad decisions but has the ability and desire to change.

At one point, I asked the women how many of them felt they were role models. Not a single one raised a hand. I then asked them how many had younger cousins, nieces, nephews, or their own children. Every woman raised her hand. "Have you ever been talking to a friend when a younger child was around, and the next thing you knew everything you said was repeated to you or another adult?" I asked. They all laughed and shook their heads in the affirmative.

"All of you are role models because you are modeling a role," I continued. "Positive or negative, that's *your* choice. My question for you is: Do you want to model what you did to get you in here?" Some silently and solemnly shook their heads no, while others answered the question out loud, affirming that they would choose a better path when they were on the other side of the prison walls.

What I really wanted them to "get" was that they were role models, and in some aspects of their lives they were good ones (many of them spent all their visiting hours with their children, reading and playing with them; others decided to go back to school or do something else to better their lives "on the other side"). I also wanted them to understand that when they got out they'd need safety manuals themselves—people who could show them how to stay on a straight path.

These young women had made some seriously misguided decisions that had devastating consequences. This most likely is not the place where most of you are at right now. Those living behind bars often have to traverse a long, winding road to good citizenship—but so do many law-abiding people who have lost their sense of community. Individuals are only as strong and successful as what they can offer fellow humans—right now and in the future.

Each of us can wake up tomorrow and decide to be the person who we want to be. We can all find safety people, and model them to develop an actionable understanding of our passions. Once you are modeling the best astronaut, teacher, speaker, or whatever it is you want to become, you are truly halfway there.

5. Announce Your Presence with a High-Speed Flyover

When you've become aware of your *umph,* a big picture generally emerges. I compare it to surveying the land before coming down for a landing in a helicopter. Yes, you are deliberate in your landing and much slower than a jet when you're flying (i.e., executing a mission), but you approach and survey quickly. And you can land on a dime, in the right place, at the right time. Finding your passion is the same—once you have identified it, do a flyover so you know what you're working with. People might question why you're flying in a circular pattern, but *you* know what you're doing. This gives you a chance to look over your terrain and anything else that will affect your landing: where the friendly troops are, where potholes might be located, and so on. And yes, some people will see where you're headed, and some might even lend a helping hand. At that point, you can think about "landing": planning and preparing.

The idea of announcing your intention is twofold. First, people come out of the woodwork to help you. How can anyone give you guidance, make introductions, or offer advice if they don't know what you're up to? Second, letting your objective be known is a way of holding yourself accountable for results.

Amazingly serendipitous, perfect outcomes happen when we stand up and say, "I'm an expert recipe developer," or "I make award-winning cocktails," or "I'm planning to use my skills as a photographer and open a portrait studio." It happened to me. I was sitting at my desk, still on active duty. Even a Marine needs a break, right? Well, living up to my old saying of "You have to make your break," I decided it was time to be self-prescribed. I took the elevator up to the fifth floor to visit a friend.

She wasn't at her desk, so I turned around to go back downstairs. As I walked back to the elevator, I saw my friend walking toward me with someone I had never seen before. My friend introduced me, and we started chatting. The conversation quickly turned to what I was going to do when I got out of the Marine Corps. I responded very simply and directly with my flyover response: "I am going to be a motivational speaker." We kept talking, and near the end of our conversation, the woman told me she couldn't and wouldn't make any promises, but she might have a contact for Les Brown, a world-renowned motivational speaker. I was floored.

I had just been on Les Brown's Web site a few days before, and at the time I dismissed attending his training anytime soon. The seminar was more than $2,500, and I was getting ready to be out of a paycheck. Les Brown is a major figure in the speaking world *and* very busy—how would I get a one-on-one audience with him? About a week later, my new acquaintance called with a contact name and number. Two months later, I was a student in Les Brown's hard-to-get-into speaker's seminar—and was able to talk to him person to person. He even sat me down, looked me in the eyes, and asked what he could do to help me succeed.

As I look back on that seminar today, it was an enormous catalyst for my speaking career. Les Brown got to know me—he's even endorsed me. I also met Dave Boufford, who would become one of my best friends. Some of you might know him as Mr. Positive (www.mrpositive.com). It was Dave who put me on the map by designing my original Web site and speaker video demo. That site was the link/exposure that created many of the speaking opportunities I booked at such a crucial time during my transition—leaving a steady paying job for self-employment.

Notice that when the woman asked me what I wanted to do when I got out, I didn't say, "find a civilian job related to my military expertise." Not that there would be anything wrong with that, but it would have been the "safe" answer for me. I decided to share my passion and say it out loud. And it felt good to hear the words come out of my mouth. Every time I said it, it reinforced that I was more than just driven; I was fueled by fire. It resulted in a fantastic contact that changed my life and actually allowed me to start doing what I wanted to do. Miracles are made by you.

6. *Mission Accomplished: The Eagle Has Landed*

Breakthroughs confirm our purpose and our importance in the world. Once you are conscious of your passion, you also have to be aware of when you have succeeded. Success is a sign to keep going. Mission accomplished: You've found your passion. Confirmations come continuously throughout the Z2B process. They direct you and keep you from taking the wrong route by separating productive missions from unproductive ones.

One of my missions in Iraq was flying five hundred feet off the ground over a hostile country—more than seven thousand miles from my family, friends, and loved ones. It was hotter than hot (95 degrees is considered a cool breeze in the Arab desert), and the combat intensity matched the 123-degree air temperature.

One of our aircraft had been shot down a few days prior. The air controller on the ground had informed us that a squad of Marines and soldiers were pinned down by mortar fire; rockets lobbed in a high arc through the air. They were in grave danger because they had no ammunition to fire back at the enemy position; they didn't even have any smoke to mark their position for us. Marines never give up: They signaled us with a small mirror. Once I spotted their location, the controller gave us a description of the enemy building, a structure that had a tower with a blue dome. I found the building and saw small arms fire coming from the tower: enemy identified.

We circled back around, and I sighted the building on my target screen. My helicopter's weapons system signaled it was armed and ready to fire. However, when I pulled the trigger, nothing happened. We quickly communicated in the cockpit and reset the weapons system. I then took a deep breath and pulled the trigger again. This time it came off and I guided the shot toward the target perfectly, causing major damage to the building in a massive cloud of dust and debris. The enemy had been destroyed, and the Marines and soldiers were able to carry on with their mission.

When I got back home from that tour in Iraq to the sunny Southern California base, I started the day as I usually do. I hopped in my Jeep Wrangler with the top down, headed north on 5, and sat in bumper-to-bumper traffic. I took a wonderfully deep breath—the fumes even smelled great! It was so good to be home. I took the nearest exit and got on the Pacific Coast Highway—more bumper-to-bumper traffic. But here I could take in the scenery: waves rolling in under white puffy clouds. Palm trees swaying in the wind, sweet breeze on my cheek. It really *was* good to be home. Back on base, I completed a little paperwork and then headed over to the base hospital for a routine medical appointment. When I arrived I got in line and started doing what I love to do: talk.

I started up a conversation with a young Marine in front of me: "Hey, Marine, how're you doing, what's going on?"

"Well, ma'am, I'm here for some physical therapy."

"Physical therapy? What happened?"

"I have some shrapnel in my leg."

"Shrapnel? Were you recently deployed?"

"Yes ma'am, 11th MEU, Iraq."

"Hey," I said, "I was on the 11th MEU [Marine Expeditionary Unit]. I was your Cobra air support."

"Ma'am, you fly Cobras? I was in the cemetery, we were pinned down, we called in Cobras, and they shot a missile...."

And at this point, I'm thinking *whoa,* wait a minute... same mission, same aircraft. We paired up the days and figured out it was indeed the same mission: aircraft and missile. We started whooping and hollering in the middle of the hospital standing in line ... and we were *not* in the psych ward!

"I'm the pilot who pulled the trigger," I said.

He stopped and looked at me. After a noticeable pause, he said, "Ma'am, you saved my life."

At that moment, the belief in my passion and mission crystallized. I knew that my passion to protect and serve had led me to the right career choice. And proof was standing right in front of me—a young, brave guy with his whole life in front of him. I knew from firsthand experience how his family, his buddies, and his sweetheart were feeling. A little shrapnel is nothing when you're talking about life versus death. I was humbled—and grateful—beyond belief. Most important, that young man was the physical confirmation of my chosen path. For a period in my life, I chose to serve and protect, and right there, standing in front of me was one of the many beautiful results of that decision.

The paths we choose lead us down some remarkable roads that are rarely seen from our starting point, and often don't make an appearance until we've traveled many miles over days, weeks, and even years. That's one of the magical results of going from Zero to Breakthrough. You end up in the most amazing places.

BREAK POINT CASE STUDY: EXPLORE YOUR OPTIONS AND LOOK SO YOU CAN LEAP

We all know most normal college freshmen are extra-excited about one thing: partying! As a college freshman with no money, I still wanted to "rec-re-ate," right? With that in mind, I always had my eye out for the possibility of a cool adventure. One day, as I was walking down the hall in the student union building, I spotted a flyer on the wall that read FREE TRIP TO MARDI GRAS. My eyes got big, and I ran over to the flyer thinking, "Wow, now this is for me!" As I got closer, I saw there was a little more to read— one line of small print at the bottom. All I had to do was join the Women's ROTC rifle team. My excitement quickly evaporated.

The military was the last thing on my mind. Sure, my family had been in the military, but that wasn't what *I* wanted to do. I thought about it for a second: "Well, Granddad and Dad (my stepdad) were Marines, and Dad (my father) was in the Army and retired as a major, and *they* turned out well. Besides, this military thing could help me get ready for the police force. Why should I let a wooden rifle stand between me and some serious partying at Mardi Gras?" And, seriously, shooting a gun was right up my adventure alley.

I signed up for the drill team, trained for three months, and headed to Mardi Gras. I had an awesome time and had found something that would help me "prepare for my passion." I still wanted to be a police officer, and I knew the physical fitness, discipline, and military demands of the ROTC would help me out in what I was trying to do.

As you can tell by now, I always take whatever I do to the extreme. I wanted a lot more action, so I decided to join the Army Reserves. That way I could still get the training I needed and stay in school. I enlisted in the Delayed Entry Program in August 1992, and was on the bus headed for Basic Training that next January. When I got back I enrolled in summer school to make up the classes I had missed while I was away. That next fall I made another life-altering decision: I enrolled in the actual Army ROTC program on campus. I knew I had tapped in to something that would give me a strategic advantage, and I was going to take every opportunity I could get my hands on. I had no clue that what happened next would truly change my life.

That next summer, I attended the Army ROTC Advanced Camp Leadership Training: six weeks in the hot sun at Fort Bragg. We were five weeks in, and it was career day. I was excited to look at anything that would involve shooting a gun or blowing something up!

In the Army as well as ROTC you have what's called a "battle buddy," and mine was on an aviation contract. She wasn't the least bit interested in combat arms, and I had no want or desire to be a pilot. Back then, a woman couldn't even do combat arms, but I didn't care. I was checking it all out—you never know what changes time will bring. I went over to the Special Forces folks, sniper platoon, and artillery, even Delta Force! There were so many jobs that women couldn't do, in fact, that I was even considering Military Police and/or ordnance jobs. Except that as an MP officer you didn't do the cool stuff, such as patrol missions and making arrests, which the enlisted guys did. Officers were stuck with paperwork, not my thing *at all*. Around 12:30 in the afternoon, reality started to settle in, and I could feel myself becoming a little discouraged. My buddy said, "Armour, can we *please* go to the aviation tent now? I think you've looked at everything else."

Sigh. Yeah, sure, we can go to the aviation tent. Under my breath I recall saying with a bit of bitterness, "Black people don't fly." Of course, we all know that's not true—Tuskegee Airmen, Bessie Coleman, Willa Brown, and so on. But still, it just wasn't in *my* reality. My friend led the way into the tent. As my vision started to clear—we were transitioning from full sun to the dim shade of a tent—I looked toward the back of the space. I couldn't believe what I was seeing: a black chick in a flight suit!

"Why didn't I think of that?" I almost screamed! My battle buddy was staring at me as if I were crazy. "What do you mean, haven't I been telling you all along that I am going to be a pilot?" I hadn't been open to all of my options, and I had only been hurting myself. It just hadn't resonated with me until the moment I saw somebody that looked like me, that the idea of flying was the best idea in the world for me!

Folks, it all boils down to access and exposure. What are we exposed to? What are we exposing our youth to? What are you being exposed to on the job? I now call the experience of seeing that woman in the tent the *tangibility of the possibility*. How many kids, children of color in particular, wanted to play tennis before Venus and Serena, golf before Tiger Woods? Probably a lot of little kids out there are now thinking, "You know, I could even be president."

In the 2008 presidential campaign, we had Hillary Clinton, Sarah Palin, Barack Obama, and John McCain all running. A presidential race never looked quite like that before. Every boy and girl now knows there are no barriers to even the highest office in the nation. We are living in an amazing world, and the opportunities are truly limitless if we recognize them. *You can be anything,* as long as you are open to figuring out what your thing is.

Zero to Breakthrough requires an open mind, and we need to give ourselves a chance to really see what's out there that is related—even precariously—to our passions, missions, and instincts. Let's break down what I did:

1. **Kept my dream alive:** I never stopped wanting to be a police officer throughout my life.
2. **Remained focused on my mission:** Not only that, I put it into words—"I want to help my community. Something needs to be done, and I can make an impact." "I want to learn how to blow things up, use a gun, and save people." (Hey, I've got to be honest, right?)
3. **Seized opportunities that fit my mission:** And that included having fun, too, along with joining the Army and ROTC.
4. **Went back to zero:** By refusing to consider aviation as a career, I took some backward steps. I did, however, realize what I had done before it was too late.
5. **Opened my eyes to possibility:** I finally agreed to enter the aviation tent, and that changed everything: breakthrough.

It's not just people who lose sight of their passion or overlook opportunities to pursue them, because the connection between an opportunity and a goal is not always obvious. Companies do it, too, which is why Z2B can be so helpful for teams to balance vision (an eye on parallel and future trends) and mission (a focus on doing what they do best).

BREAK POINT CASE STUDY:
GETTING BACK TO THE GRIND

When I talk to large companies, I often use their mission statement as a jumping-off point. Has their mission actually changed, or has the firm's or department's responses to market conditions failed? Funny thing I've noticed—when market or other conditions shift, some companies tend to change course in a way that alters the core mission. I think that's a mistake most of the time. I believe in flexibility and adaptability. But be careful if you are going to venture away from the very mission that people believe in you for.

In the military, as in football and law enforcement, you are constantly bombarded with moves from the opponent, the weather, or other outside forces that are meant to disarm you, either by design or by sheer natural force (sometimes literally, as in war and fighting crime). Professionals in these areas are trained to respond to change without losing sight of the goal—capture the enemy, save buddies or citizens. Shifting strategy does not mean straying from the original principle. Often it means sticking with the initial plan and tweaking it to suit outside forces.

Take my morning coffee. The only cup of joe that's better than my mom's is a Starbucks. Both cups get me rockin' and rollin'. But I can't expect Mom to brew a pot on demand every day. (She'd do it because she's a darling, but I won't let her.)

I was standing in line at Starbucks a while ago and felt like something was different. I looked around and didn't see anything that stood out. We all know that if you've been in one Starbucks, you've pretty much been in them all—and somehow that's comforting. I know that every time I ordered my White Chocolate Mocha, it would be just as good as the last time. The same things would be on the menu, and as soon as I hit the door I'd smell the crisp, deep aroma of coffee beans. That was it! That's what was missing! The experience.

It wasn't the same Starbucks I had come to know and love—it was turning into a run-of-the-mill coffee shop. I went there not only because the coffee was happening, but the whole experience of watching a barista grind the beans, prepare the potion, and serve it with style made the hot cup of get-up-and-go seem all the more delicious. The coffee was now prebrewed and delivered from the spigot of a big tank. Like any fast-food place. Like gas. Was it me, or did the cup I had in my hand taste sort of burnt, and not really fresh? The workers didn't seem all that enthusiastic about pushing the spigot either. Starbucks was even selling *instant* coffee. Say what?

I was not surprised in the least when I read in the business section of my local newspaper that Starbucks had hit a rough patch. Growth had stalled; same store sales were down by 9 percent, and more than one thousand stores were going to be shuttered. The stock price was in a two-year decline, or maybe freefall, since it was hovering near $10, off from a high of $30 in 2007. At the same time, the company had been introducing new products that didn't seem to enhance the brand: tea lattes and, as I mentioned, VIA, an instant coffee. Is VIA Sanka for celebrities? With the Starbucks original brew "experience" eroding, and the company pushing freeze-dried granules off as a viable beverage, for me Starbucks had lost its mojo—and its mission: to serve freshly brewed coffee made by hand and to order in a unique coffeehouse-type setting.

A few years ago, then chairman Howard Schultz wrote a letter to the company's executives blaming the cheapened coffee-shop experience he had championed on management's focus on excessive growth and efficiency. Mr. Schultz wrote that the switch to preground, prebrewed coffee had taken the "romance and theater" out of a trip to Starbucks—and that's what people were willing to pay extra for. I certainly was. "We achieved fresh-roasted bagged coffee, but at what cost? The loss of aroma—perhaps the most powerful nonverbal signal we had in our stores," he wrote. Starbucks, once a leading brand, had plunged back to zero when they started to step away from their original *umph*: brewing a consistent, small luxury coffee in a relaxed, efficient environment.

Some time later, I read that the company had instituted a series of changes in the hope of refocusing on its original mission to provide an "experiential beverage" as a way to win back customers and address increased competition from McDonald's McCafé and even 7-Eleven. For example, instead of grinding coffee only in the morning, baristas will grind beans each time a new pot is brewed. I can now hear the whir of grinders and smell the aroma of fresh coffee all day, just like I used to. By taking a critical look at their situation, Starbucks was able to get back to their original passion and back to their original success.

Let's break down the Zero to Breakthrough method for finding passion as played out by the actions of Starbucks:

1. **Realized they were stalled:** Recognizing a problem is the first step in correcting it. They were at zero.

2. **Tried to solve loss of customer interest and competition issues by copying cheaper brands:** That didn't work, and the company knew they had to go back to the drawing board immediately.

3. **Looked at their mission, and recognized cheapening the brand was a bad idea:** It did not fit in at all with the expectations of the customer, which was to have an almost bespoke, or "custom," coffee experience.

4. **Made the tough decision to close stores in underperforming locations:** Starbucks turned the focus to their most successful stores.

5. **Restated the Starbucks mission:** They provide a unique customer experience.

6. **Made changes that eliminated the coffee outages that lost business:** Starbucks provided a new way to make their original mission work using relatively inexpensive new technology that allowed an efficient return to batch grinding and brewing.

7. **Increased store sales—breakthrough:** People who are looking for "affordable luxuries" are giving Starbucks another chance.

KEEP TRACK OF ZERO TO BREAKTHROUGH MOMENTS TO DISCOVER YOUR ABILITIES

One of the reasons why people might feel intimidated by the idea of Zero to Breakthrough is that they don't see it as a possibility in their lives. It just seems too big. Yet you are having Zero to Breakthrough moments all the time—one was to realize you needed a jumpstart to begin with! I use three awareness techniques that can create more of these moments: record, write, and remember.

Mindfulness of little breakthroughs is essential. Staying aware gives you proof positive that you already have the ability to go from Zero to Breakthrough. It also allows you to examine these triumphs and build on them. What made you do these things, and how did they make you feel? How exactly did the breakthrough happen? Can you repeat the basic steps that got you there by applying them consciously to bigger dreams?

I always make sure to *record* important conversations and reexamine them later. I'm polite and honest and let the person know (especially if it is a phone conversation) that my tape is running, and no one has ever said no. For instance, when I have an important brainstorming session with a colleague or friend, I record it and listen to it later for ideas, talking points, and key words I might have missed in "real time" or didn't write down. I listen carefully to my own delivery as a way of perfecting my public presentations. How many times have you said something, and then had to stop to say, "Hey, that was good!" or "Did I just say that? Let me write that down!" The point of this exercise is to develop your own mental practice of listening, questioning, learning, and revealing.

Recording helped me with the name "Zero to Break-through." I was working with a friend, Ellen Kaminsky, on my elevator speech. Ellen gives people clarity, and that's just what I needed! By the end of our three-hour session, I was mentally exhausted. "I just want you to capture the essence of what I'm trying to say and be. Acceleration, speed, passion, breaking personal sound barriers," I said. "Imagine you are the Space Shuttle. One second you are sitting at zero on the pad, ninety-one seconds later you're orbiting Earth." Ellen quickly said, "Well, Vernice, think about it. You basically went from zero, not to say being a cop is nothing, but zero to being America's first African-American female combat pilot. You went from zero to breakthrough. And look at how you tackle everything in your life."

My breath was taken away and goose bumps had taken its place as we both realized what she had just said. I jumped up in amazement and yelled out in the middle of the restaurant, "That's it! Zero to Breakthrough!" Amazingly enough, I had recorded the entire conversation; if I hadn't, I wouldn't have been able to recall much of what was said after that, as excited as I was. Turns out some pretty deep ideas were exchanged, and I had recorded them, too! I listened to that recording just a few days ago, and even after all that time I got goose bumps right when I knew she was getting ready to say those words. And I have to admit that I even get a little misty-eyed. I'm listening to a moment of birth—what a miraculous blessing.

Writing also gives me a chance to jot down observations and bright ideas wherever I am. Have you ever been driving in the car when lightning strikes in your brain? Hold that thought and write it down as soon as you can. I journal every day and record the day's thoughts, events, and encounters. My journal is now an important testimony of the past few years—one that I refer to and am frequently inspired by.

Finally, I *remember* my breakthrough moments by tracking them. You might even want to dedicate a pad or journal to your breakthrough moments. The more you list, the more encouraged you'll be. I guarantee you'll be floored by how many times you have a breakthrough once you take the time to notice when it happens. And when you're feeling low or having a hard time drumming up gratitude, reflecting on previous breakthrough moments is a reminder of how great your life really is.

Z2B EXERCISE: START YOUR ENGINES

I can't end this chapter without sharing an exercise that helps many people get moving toward their *umph*:

Make time for a daily fifteen- to thirty-minute honest reflection. This may seem like a lot of time for a busy person, but it really isn't. You won't be doing nothing; you will be learning and discovering. So stop making excuses. The subconscious is always working on the questions that you are asking yourself.

Cut off distractions (TV, radio, Internet, e-mail, kids, spouse, roommates), and take yourself and your mind into an "isolation chamber" (even if it's the bathroom). Gaze at the stars, take a walk in nature, journal, get into a meditative yoga pose, or simply find that quiet space, relax, and close your eyes (but don't fall asleep). Instead of forcing yourself to "think hard" about your true calling, let your mind drift. Focus on the ultimate outcome and the impact you want it to have on your life. Write down what empowers you and what makes you feel good, strong, and alive.

It's amazing how letting go results in deep insights and clarity. Twenty, thirty, forty, maybe even fifty or sixty years from now, when you're sitting on your front porch looking back on your life, what legacy do you want to have? What imprint do you wish to have left on the world? I can guarantee you won't be sitting there wishing you had spent more hours at your desk working or that you'd worked more Saturdays.

When I started journaling and reflecting, I began by just writing down anything that came into my mind— pretty loose and unconstructed, as you might imagine. Through that stream-of-consciousness process, I realized that I had many great ideas that would not have materialized had I not taken the time to let myself go. In turn, when I applied my system to these ideas, they turned into breakthroughs. For instance, I was able to book my first few speaking engagements; I created a business strategy based on Zero to Breakthrough; I was able to get in touch with people who would help and advise me.

When I thought about the book you have in your hands, my quiet time and free-range journaling helped me enumerate the things I needed to do to reach book breakthrough. I felt very empty and was afraid I'd run out of ideas. I had so many questions and no answers. Then I started to work on ideas for a series of short books on specific subjects I wanted to speak on, and that lead to an idea for a book based on Zero to Breakthrough. That's when I came to the realization that with my book ideas, I was not stuck, I just wasn't moving. Journaling helped me work out a plan:

1. Just start writing. Close the journal, start the book. Done.
2. Find out what I need to do to publish a book: create a strong, concise concept; reach out to literary agents; find someone to help me organize my ideas (I'm a Marine, not Ernest Hemingway); get it sold!
3. Continue to add speaking engagements and new clients to my roster.
4. Continue networking.

Yes, all of this came from quiet time. Thirty minutes, an hour, two hours—I am telling you that you have the time for this, and it is time worth taking.

Z2B EXERCISE: MAKE A STATEMENT

Let's end the chapter with our passions in place. Once you have identified your passion and purpose, you've found your *umph*. Write it down and place the statement where you can see it every day (your bathroom, fridge, bedroom, computer). Seeing your passion in writing is a powerful reminder to keep yourself focused. The mission has just begun.

Always Faithful

The Marines have a motto, *semper fidelis*, or "always faithful." That should be your motto as you go from Zero to Breakthrough: Stay true to your talents, passions, and values and you rarely will be at a loss for solutions. If it means regularly reengaging with your stated mission and purpose, so be it. Loyalty to goals and respect for your talents are two of the secrets of creating a life around purpose. There's more to breakthrough than simply being faithful to your dreams. Once you've made the commitment to go from Zero to Breakthrough, you have to start planning. In the next chapter, we'll dig deeply into the research and development phase.

FLY-AWAYS

- Stop making excuses.

- Dream like a child.

- Notice when you're deeply engaged.

- Reframe your now and make it about tomorrow.

- Model your future through your behavior today.

- Shout your purpose from the rooftops (or at least tell people about it).

- Look for confirmation.

- Make time for contemplation.

- Write down your passion so you can see it every day.

CHAPTER 2

Set and Ready: Preparation and Procrastination

> *Nothing succeeds in war except*
> *in consequence of a well-prepared plan.*
>
> —NAPOLEON BONAPARTE

As I prepared to drive the six hours from Columbus, Ohio, to Nashville to take the second test toward becoming a police officer, I made sure I knew the best route *before* I pulled out of the driveway. It's a fairly straight shot down to Nashville from Columbus. Still, I wanted to be certain there would be no construction going on that could delay my arrival. After a bit of online research, I called some friends who had the 411 on local roads and planned my route accordingly.

When I got behind the wheel, I was secure in the knowledge that I'd make it to the test on time. I-71 and I-65, which made up the bulk of the trip, were free and clear, and I was aware of the detour I had to take when I hit I-264. No journey is ever complete without a surprise or two. Why not count on that fact, and stay ready? After all, this trip was part of the path, *literally*, to my then-passion!

This straightforward example of plan and prep is a crisp, simple model for any kind of journey—whether it's a car trip or a climb up the corporate ladder. When we navigate the always-unpredictable road to our purpose and passion, it helps to have a strategy, road map, flight plan, or system. Call it whatever you want; the proper groundwork sets us up for success and helps us deal with setbacks more easily—or at least without doing unintentional damage. You know the old saying: If you fail to prepare, prepare for failure.

Plan and prep not only makes it easier to start a project by answering the question, "Where do I begin;" it provides a sense of calm and order so we can take decisive action if we have to, especially when faced with a critical or unpredictable situation. Planning and preparation are, in fact, essential ingredients for having meaningful breakthroughs.

Trying to skip planning, and "fly by the seat of your pants" often results in failure, disappointment, and surrender, not to mention time wasted. Working with individuals and groups at companies and organizations has helped me zero in on the four most common reasons why people don't start the Zero to Breakthrough plan and prep phase:

1. *Fear of crashing.* We think we'll fail—anxiety over not doing something well circles us right back to square one.

2. *Postponing.* We procrastinate because we think we'll fail, and/or we don't know where to start.

3. *Ignorance.* We require additional knowledge about our chosen plan that we have yet to attain.

4. *Confusion.* We're already on the road when we realize we have no plan, and it shows.

Fortunately, these issues can be overcome with Zero to Breakthrough mojo—and that includes active effort on your part. Remember, where there's no sweat there's no magic. The organizations I have had the privilege of belonging to, the ROTC, the Nashville Police Department, the San Diego Sunfire, the Tempe Police Department, and the United States Marine Corps all had one important thing in common: They all took preparation seriously. Which was a good thing, since each of these dangerous professions carried a potentially heavy price tag—my life. By the time I was through with training and practice, I was confident and ready for what I might encounter on the field, on the streets, or in the sky. But I'm getting ahead of myself.

CRASH FAILURE

Failure is fertilizer.

—LADONNA GATLIN

While I firmly believe that failure is not a destination, I know that "win/win or no deal" may be tough hero's talk in theory, but it's an attitude that allows little room for risk or experimentation. The problem with an all or nothing outlook ("I am not going to climb the mountain unless I can get to the top") is that when things look like they are going south, you might be tempted to quit early on just to avoid a loss—and this can happen, and often does, in the planning stage. It's like being too scared to look—if you start to plan and discover complexities you hadn't seen when you were still in the dreaming stage, you might get cold feet ("Wow, you mean I might get hypothermia up there—forget it!").

Marine training showed me that planning is a learning tool that helps you sharpen your judgment and anticipate problems before you confront them "in the field," and it's not just a mechanical process that's done the same way every time. Most important of all, planning steers people *away* from potential failure while simultaneously preparing them for it. Former Marine Robert Kiyosaki wrote in his book *Rich Dad, Poor Dad*, "The greatest secret of winners is that failure inspires winning; thus, they're not afraid of losing." A Marine perspective goes something like this: Failure is often a necessary predecessor to success.

Let's lay it on the line and get it out of the way: You *will* fail. Even with excellent planning and preparation, it can and will happen. So what? So great! Failures are opportunities. The faster we fail, the faster we can succeed. Some people call this phenomenon Failure Bounce. Think of a basketball. When Kobe Bryant hits one to the floor, it reaches its lowest point when it meets the court floor—the harder it smacks down, the more speed it gains on the way up. It accelerates exponentially from that impact. It's energized. That ball can be you.

I failed the flight test on the first try and passed it on the second. I sought out every study guide I could find and dug in for a month, took the test, and passed with flying colors.

I also didn't get accepted to Officer Candidate School until my third submission. Before that, when I wanted to join the Army, I showed up for the exam and was rejected because I was slightly overweight. The officer asked me if I could lose ten pounds in two weeks, and I said yes. I worked my butt off (literally) and in two weeks had lost ten pounds. That was some fierce bounce! Breakthrough: I was athlete of the year at Camp Pendleton and a two-time winner of the base's Strongest Warrior Competition. What you do with failure—how you choose to respond to it—is key to having breakthroughs. I could have laid down my arms at any point out of disappointment, anger, or frustration, but I didn't.

First, I rarely engage in self-criticism. This doesn't mean I don't see myself for who I am, flaws and all. I'm always working on improving myself. But I don't talk myself down, especially when I've made a mistake or didn't reach a goal the first time around. There are people who are stifled by negative self-talk. They cannot seem to stop the bad news loop from running in their heads. A financial advisor I know is filled with doubt when a client calls for guidance: *What if I give them bad advice? What if they lose their shirts because of me? How dare I call myself a financial expert?* She's always afraid to take on new clients, and she's overly careful—even though she's an astute judge of the markets.

I know lots of athletes, and most of them are confident; their naturally competitive spirit allows for Failure Bounce. Yet every once in a while I meet a runner or body builder who has self-doubt. A competitive runner loses a race and thinks: *Total loser.*

I should give up running and do something else. That thinking feeds on itself, and the runner has a losing streak for months.

If your inner voice is putting you down and scaring you away, there are three Z2B strategies you can use to quiet it down and shift your thinking.

1. *Catch yourself doing something well.* Instead of observing every time you think you've screwed up—and mentioning it to yourself—make a mental note of your successes and turn the criticism tape on its head: *Good job, girl! You really topped yourself that time.*

2. *Ask yourself, "Are you serious?"* When you talk down to yourself it's generally out of proportion to reality. We can get pretty hard on ourselves. Think about the precision of what you're saying: *"I can't add two and two," "No way I'll ever be able to finish that report in twenty-four hours; if I do it won't be very good."* Are these statements true or are they exaggerations? If they are true, what can you do to change? If not, start being honest and reasonable about what you can and can't do, and work on the stuff you have control over.

3. *Realize that sometimes things just are what they are.* Everything that "goes wrong" in your life does not have deep cosmic meaning; and is not always your fault, predictable, or possible to change. So instead of thinking, *"What's wrong with me, why can't I make more sales this month?"* try this: *"The economy is really tough; I can't change it, but I can change my sales pitch to fit the tough times."* In short, depersonalize the world. It's not all about you.

POSTPONE AND PROCRASTINATE

I do it. We all do. I'll spend an extra few minutes chatting with my mom in the morning, and she can easily talk me into having another cup of coffee with her. I'll put off reading important paperwork until the evening, when I'm really too tired to concentrate. So it gets placed on the next day's to-do list. These are the day-to-day rain checks that, in the scheme of things, probably don't hurt us too much (when is spending a few extra minutes with Mom not a good thing?).

As of this writing, my goal is to win or place in a body-building competition, and I am in the midst of trying to prepare for my first contest in November. I should be working out regularly and losing a certain amount of weight each month. Yet with just six months to go, I haven't been putting in 100 percent effort. It's ironic, because I used to be a gym rat, even sneaking away from my job to work out. Now that I have the time, I haven't been going and I'll take any excuse not to put in even forty-five minutes of work.

What's up with that? Procrastination. Some of my hesitance is based in reality. I'm concerned that I no longer have the strength and stamina to compete in an extremely challenging physical endeavor—after all, I'm not twenty-five anymore. Maybe so, but why wouldn't I just go ahead and find out? I'm healthy and strong, and still in my thirties. There's no physical reason why I can't compete and do well, even if I don't come in first place. I've got to remind myself that while first place might be nice, it's not always necessary or possible for me right now. That does not mean I shouldn't try.

When we delay and defer the work that goes into our big

dreams and important passions—well, that's when we find ourselves twenty years down the line wondering why we're still doing a job we don't like or living in a home or a town that brings us down. "Coulda, shoulda" becomes a way of life.

The trick to starting is doing something—anything—that puts you in the general direction of your goal. You know, like the Nike ad says: *Just do it.* I say, *Just do something, anything, now.* Okay, people ask me, "Cleaning out my sock drawer can help me organize a cross-country bike trip?" or "Spending an hour in the library is really going to score me a job as a chef?" Yes, and yes. You don't eat an elephant in one bite. You have to take a lot of small bites over time (to avoid indigestion) to finish the job. Every small nibble gets you closer to the finish line as long as you keep munching away.

Getting started has a lot to do with momentum—having even a little is like adding a sprinkle of yeast to warm water and sugar. The mixture expands, bubbles, and rises. Momentum comes from excitement and enthusiasm, which can be supplied by others (people can be your yeast) or by your own actions that are designed to inspire and energize. A Breakthrough Buddy (BTB) can help motivate you—mine has agreed to nag me (yup, permission granted) and follow up to make sure I put in some time at the gym every day. I'm getting there.

So how do we break out of a patch of procrastination? Review, Recharge, and Reattack.

1. *Review.* I took a step back the other day and looked at what was really going on: I (of all people) might be lacking in confidence over whether I could win a

competition with so many more experienced people on stage. I reminded myself that I had beat out a more experienced pilot when I was assigned the Cobra helicopter as a Marine. Recently I was able to bench press a weight I thought I'd never attain. Believe me, I gave myself a pat on the back for that one (as soon as I put the barbells down, of course). That achievement, along with my BTB's high-five, encouraged me to keep up the good work.

2. *Recharge.* This is simply taking steps that assist your enthusiasm so you can renew your own efforts spiritually, physically, and intellectually. For me it was as simple and relaxing as creating a vision board with photos of women body builders I admire and aspire to look like. It's posted prominently in my bedroom, so I see those amazing women every morning and evening. I can't get away from them! I also attend bodybuilding contests on a fairly regular basis, which reminds me of where I am going come November. I can also study what goes on, learn from other contestants' mistakes, and be inspired by all of those women who are making the effort to achieve. I say to myself, "This is where I am trying to go," and then I make a commitment to my commitment.

3. *Reattack.* Okay, we're all going back in! With the help of my BTB, I put my workouts on my calendar, just like any important business appointment. That way I knew the time was blocked out and I would not double book by mistake. I called a friend and told her what I was

doing, and she promised to call me before and after my workout to support me and to make sure I actually followed through with it. I found a personal trainer to motivate and train me—since I'm paying an hourly rate for his services, there is no way I'm going to stand him up.

This three-pronged plan is similar to the preparation I made when I wanted to become a police officer. After I had completed a considerable amount of research and study, I had reached the test-taking phase. After taking and passing the initial test to become a police officer, I waited an entire year to hear that I qualified for final testing. During those twelve months, I never lost hope, or my objective. I mentally claimed my spot on the police force and I took the necessary steps to get there. Accepting the challenges and responsibilities I needed to progress ensured that there would be no excuses and no backing down when the time for the final test came.

I got in shape (lifting weights and running), so I was confident that any physical demands the job required would be easily met. The Police Academy was going to be physically challenging, at least it would be if it were anything like ROTC Basic Training. I have to admit, there were times when I was one of the last recruits to finish a run, but I knew as long as I didn't quit and gave it my all, I would be making progress toward my goal. At the end of the six months, my preparation paid off, and about a year later I became the first black female to make the Nashville police motorcycle squad and its second female to ride a motorcycle.

THERE'S NO BLISS WITH IGNORANCE

When I speak to young people, I always ask them what they want to do when they grow up. They shout out answers energetically: "pro ball player," "chef," "astronaut," "veterinarian," and so on. My very next question is, "How do you get there?" This question usually stumps them—"practice" or "go to school" are their typical generic responses. It's hard for boys and girls to go into detail because few ever dig deeply into their "destination." Unfortunately, many adults think this way, too. Maybe it's the instant gratification world we live in, but we seem to have lost the urge to look before we leap.

The day I signed up for each of my professions—the military, law enforcement, and pro sports—I knew exactly what to expect. I had done the research about what was required of each role and what was expected in terms of professional behavior, education, and duties. Once inside, my first order of business was to understand and respect the systems that already were in place. As a police officer recruit, for example, I trained on the gun range, not to become good at hitting the center of a paper target but to prepare for the possibility of facing a situation in which I needed to fire a weapon with precision.

When I made it to the advanced flight school training phase in the Marines, I wanted to fly Cobras, but so did the only captain in our class. Here I was, a second lieutenant going up against a captain for a Cobra slot. After my lesson in primary, when I had failed to make it into the top group to become a jet fighter pilot, I knew I had to graduate first in my class in Marine Aviation if I was going to earn the Cobra. Rumor had it there would only be one Cobra slot for our class. It's the biggest, baddest helicopter around, so second place wasn't an option. If I were to party or watch TV too much, or just goof off, the captain who was studying to beat me would indeed beat me.

After my last experience, I didn't need any convincing that I had to get serious. My very dreams were on the line. I had never studied so intensely in my life—even harder than when I studied for the Marine flight test. The considerable amount of research I had done well before the test, along with studying manuals and lessons, had paid off. I had also prepared myself by getting in shape (lifting weights and running) to make sure I was ready physically. And I was honest with myself—flying a Cobra was "sexy," but it also was deadly. The purpose of it was ultimately to protect troops on the ground and kill the enemy when necessary. If flying a Cobra was anything like Army Basic Training or being a beat cop, I knew it was going to take my mind, body, and soul beyond the limits of their capabilities.

After the test was over, I felt pretty good about how I'd done, though there was the question of the guy who outranked me. When it came down to selection day, my eleven classmates and I were standing around in the hall outside the classroom awaiting our fate. The instructors had written the names of twelve different aircrafts on the board in the classroom: The first person called into the room could choose whichever one they wanted; the last guy to walk into the classroom took whatever was left on the board. I knew the number one slot was between the captain and me. We were pretending not to eye each other nervously as we waited in the hall.

The instructors came out and looked at all of us, then

looked at me and said, "Come on, Vee, we know you want the Cobra, what coast do you want?" I was ecstatic, and everyone could see it (no sense trying to act cool, calm, and collected). I had accomplished my goal—the work and planning had paid off big time. I was going to be a Cobra pilot.

There were many things I learned "on the job" as a Cobra pilot, just like there were things I learned as a cop and a football player after I had started in those jobs. Everyone learns more about what they do as they do it. There's a difference between intellectual knowledge and practical experience. Yet there was no way I would have had good experiences or could have handled tough situations in the military had I not had a lot of information, training, and practice going in. It's just not a good idea to walk through a door without knowing something about what's on the other side.

GO ON A FACT-FINDING MISSION

Find out everything you can about your passion—the good, the bad, and the unexpected. Be honest—always get at the truth. That way you can anticipate the challenges ahead and plan for them. Preparatory research leads to innovation—the more you know the more likely you are to discover new ways of achieving goals and reaching a true breakthrough moment. Dr. Samuel Betances of the Workforce Diversity Institute once told me something important about knowledge. Maybe it was the simple way he put it, but the words have stayed with me. As Betances sees it, humans started out in the age of "hardware." We hunted and gathered, then plowed and worked in the fields.

We then moved on to the age of "hardware," the industrial age. We used heavy machinery, the assembly line was created, and many people were working in urban factories instead of with their hands in the fields.

Combat Confidence: Identify what you don't know about your passion so you can fill in the blanks. Even then, acknowledge that you don't know everything. Being humble helps you stay open to new information and better ways of doing things.

Today, we have moved away from handware and hardware into the age of "headware." Betances is talking about intellectual property; it's what's in your head that's going to take you places today. You have to be serious about your education as it relates to your dreams. Even if you are going into a physically demanding profession, or are after a dream that will bring you in contact with the land, with handware and hardware, intellectual capital is important because natural resources and technology are now inextricably linked.

All education isn't *necessarily* formal, classroom learning. Naturally, part of preparation is finding out not only what you need to know—but the best way to know it as well. For the aspiring scholar, the ivy halls of the university are just the place, yet for the basketball or football player who wants a place on a pro team, consistent practice is also serious education. Finding a mentor who can relay certain moves and techniques is also important. The mind meets the hand in situations like these. For the would-be chef, cooking is key. Apprenticing in a restaurant kitchen is your college. Working as a line cook is graduate school.

Understanding and learning from the masters and knowing the rules is the only way to break them and make something new and delicious. The best way to get going is to devote some time every day to your passion. Any amount of time will do—thirty minutes, an hour, or an afternoon—as long as you're consistent. For example:

Ask for help and advice from people who are already doing what you want to do.

You can pick the experts' brains anytime in the prep and plan stage. First of all, it's inspiring to talk to someone who loves what he or she does. That alone can be the yeast you need to create momentum. It's also a very good way to build up contacts. As you move forward, closer to your goal, you're also building a network.

Cultivate the spirit of discovery.

Think of the preparation stage as an adventure—it is. You know the old saying about how it's not the destination; it's the journey that's so great. It's true only if you make it so. Go on a fact-finding mission to locate the best of the best in your field. Theirs are the shoulders you'll stand on. Devote time to Internet research, reading, and visiting people and places related to your cause. Ask one of your experts if you can "shadow" them for an afternoon or a couple of hours. Say you want to open a motorcycle shop (or any kind of store)—volunteer your time in one on the weekends, befriend the owner, and learn everything you can about how he or she runs the business.

Get some wingmen (or women).

Lieutenant Colonel Rob "Waldo" Waldman, a fellow speaker and friend, talks about the importance of your wingman. Surround yourself with people who understand your passion and support your cause. In military-speak, these are pilots who position their aircraft outside and behind (on the wing of) the leader of a flying formation. They offer protection and cover your blind spots. They are valuable in life, too, because they encourage your endeavor and let you know if they see something coming at you that might not be in your best interests.

WHEN THE GOING GETS TOUGH, THE TOUGH HAVE A PLAN (OR HOW TO AVOID CHAOS AND CONFUSION)

Between March and May of 2003, Major James Ruvalcaba and I were a flight team—in fact, he flew 90 percent of his missions with me. He always said flying the Cobra was the best mission in the Marine Corps. Ruvalcaba and I spent a lot of time in that cockpit together. I knew his habits and he knew mine. Sometimes we were in the cockpit from sunup to sundown. Our longest mission in Iraq lasted about twenty-one hours. During flights he would mentor me on being a Marine, an investor, and a positive energy in the world. That's one of the reasons why I liked being this forty-something ex–Huey pilot's partner. Plus he had my back for sure.

Before one mission over Baghdad, we started the day as we usually did, counting down for all the aircraft to start up and do a "radio check." One of those key times is when the pilot has locked on to a target and is ready to fire. The copilots view targets in two different ways—by looking at a mini television screen or by looking "heads down" into the telescopic sight unit (TSU). As long as the missiles were looking for their target, they were considered to be in good form.

So we tested the rockets but didn't shoot them. We checked the TOW missile to see whether the correct symbols came up to indicate it was enabled and ready to fire. When I locked on to a mock target with a Hellfire, a circle with a plus sign inside appeared on an overlay. Just right. A steady, nonflashing plus sign inside the circle indicated that I had symbology (a term used to describe the symbols that show up on the weapons system when it is turned on and/or engaged) and was ready to fire my weapon.

I put the missile in Lock-On Before Launch (LOBL) mode to squirt out the laser energy and ensure that the seeker head on the Hellfire was moving around and scanning for laser energy. I configured my weapons system so that if we were attacked, all we had to do was flip a switch to arm and shoot. The team always spoke through our weapons checks, and this turned out to be great reinforcement when it came to communicating during crisis moments.

By 5:30 a.m., just as the sun was starting to come up, four

Cobras taxied down the flight line in preparation for takeoff. Ruvalcaba and I were in the third one. When we were in the air, we moved into formation, with the lead aircraft determining the speed, altitude, route, and tactical formation (or position in space) for everyone to follow.

Ruvalcaba was in the backseat, as usual, so he could control the aircraft and put it just where he wanted it. I sat in the front, navigating my section, calling out targets, and operating the weaponry. Troops were on the road to Baghdad, and we were going to provide protection for them as they headed north farther into enemy territory. We had a good idea where Regimental Combat Team 5 (RCT-5) was located on Highway 6 based on information received from the aircraft that had just been providing them with cover. With the guidance of Crusty, the regiment's forward air controller (FAC), and sometimes without his direction, because he wasn't a mind reader and didn't always know what lay ahead, we were ready to encounter an enemy laying in wait as the Marines on the ground forged ahead.

As soon as we arrived in the area of the RCT, the lead aircraft spotted a tank and an ammunition storage site. Having these ammunition dumps along the side of the road posed a threat to the troops by allowing the insurgents to rearm themselves during conflicts. They had to be destroyed. Major James Szepesy (aka Snoop) called an attack on the tank and the storage site.

Ruvalcaba and I provided support for Szepesy just in case his TOW missile went stupid or missed its target. When a missile goes stupid, it leaves the aircraft but doesn't take the guidance signals from the Cobra. So instead of heading toward its target, it just dives to the ground about two hundred feet in front of the helicopter. A dud doesn't even leave the aircraft when the copilot pulls the trigger.

Our aircraft and our wingman flew about two hundred yards to the right in trail of Snoop's section. From this vantage, we would be able to see any pop-up targets that might shoot at the first section. This formation ended up looking like an upside-down checkmark.

The strong, acrid smell of gunpowder seeped into the cockpit and stung our nostrils—par for the course when you're dropping bombs meant to destroy enemy equipment. After our division was cleared by Crusty to fire on the tank and storage site, Ruvalcaba and I zeroed in on the targets. I looked into my TSU, picked out the targets, pulled the trigger, and fired .20 mm rounds while Ruvalcaba maneuvered the aircraft to ensure continuous fire on the tank and storage site and keep the aircraft in formation with the division. Szepesy's missile took out the tank, clearing the way for the RCT to continue forward.

Crusty directed us to fly ahead of the convoy to seek out the enemy, which was our central mission. However, the ground troops were taking small-arms fire, which meant there was a good chance the aircraft would be the target of similar fire. The same small-arms fire that bounces off the armored tanks can take down an aircraft. The lead aircraft responded that it was too risky for the Cobras to fly out ahead of the convoy.

Being in the air and having special visual aids allowed us to be able to see much farther than the ground troops. We could scan up ahead, find the enemy, and fire without being on top of the enemy and making ourselves vulnerable. The energy was building, and we could feel it. Something was about to happen.

This time, we were flying at about the height of a high-tension power line and varying our speed between 70 and 100 knots (80 to 100 mph) to avoid being shot down. We maneuvered around as we looked for the enemy, their vehicles, and their ammunition sites. It was rolling terrain with big fields on either side of the main highway. On the left side of the highway, there was a stream that meandered through the fields and had trees bordering each side of it—excellent cover for a hiding enemy. My body felt the energy and my eyes were wide open scanning the land below, as I had done many times in training. I was looking for anything that didn't "fit" or look right. Even cars driving down the road could have been loaded with a bomb set to explode when they got next to our troops. My hand was in position to fire weapons rapidly when the time came, and at this point the aircraft were shooting "weapons free." This means that if we saw the enemy, we had the authority to shoot him with the appropriate weaponry.

While searching the area, we spotted twenty-five abandoned military vehicles with Iraqi markings, medium machine guns, and ammunition strewn about the area. Some vehicles were dug in with earthen berms to protect them from anti-tank missiles. Others were positioned in such a way that they could support each other from threats coming from multiple directions. Szepesy relayed the information back to Crusty, instructing the troops to hold their ground: *Do not advance. There are armored tanks in front of you.*

My division set up for an easterly attack to destroy two of the armored personnel carriers. I visualized the attack: I would lead with .20 mm, Ruvalcaba would shoot rockets from the backseat, and I would finish up with .20 mm on the pull-off.

All the time we would keep our wingman in sight to maintain safety and coverage for the other two aircraft in the division.

We started the attack, and I could feel the Cobra leaning in, surging toward the enemy. The first rounds and rockets were shot by Szepesy's section, and our section followed. After the success of the easterly attack, the division pulled off to the south and circled to the west for another attack, avoiding Iraqi antiaircraft artillery. I looked around to see where the aircraft and ground troops were in relation to enemy tanks on the ground. I was ready to sight in on the new target set. The westerly attack took out more armored personnel carriers facing the ground troops.

The Iraqis tried to channel the Cobras into their line of fire by pouring oil into ditches, starting fires, and temporarily blinding us with heavy smoke. This forced the aircraft to one side of the highway or the battle. When we flew out of the smoke and regained awareness of our surroundings, the Iraqis aimed small-arms fire and artillery air bursts at the aircraft. All I knew was that I was protecting troops on the ground, and that was my mission regardless of the fact that other people were trying to kill me. When I was up there, I relied heavily on my training and preparation.

As our team of Cobras closed in on the city of Al Aziziyah, we spotted two squads of Saddam's elite Republican Guard sitting in ambush southwest of the city. We had been taking sporadic fire all along, but now the bursts were getting closer and closer, so close the aircraft had to abort one of the attacks. As Szepesy pulled off from another attack, his aircraft received a crippling shot that caused his gauges to fluctuate. In a matter-of-fact tone, he told the other pilots he had been hit. He and his wingman would have to return to the FARP (Forward Arming and Refueling Point).

Cobras always fly in pairs, so Dash-1 and Dash-2 left together. Ruvalcaba and I became the new Dash-1, and our wingman Dash-2. I didn't know the extent of damage to Dash-1 and whether they'd make it back to the FARP, even though it was only six miles away. Being hit can be like running out of gas when the gas station is a mile away. If you're out of gas, you're out of gas. If the transmission seizes up in a car, you stop rolling. If it quits in a helicopter, the blades stop turning, even if its engines are still running.

Our aircraft had just become the lead for the remaining assaults. Crew management and communication was one of our strong points. Ruvalcaba immediately turned our section back into the ambush. I quickly scanned for the enemy, ready for the next attack. Then I spotted a man in Iraqi uniform running, then diving headfirst into a ditch along the river. He was trying to take cover while the enemy shot heavy small-arms and medium-caliber antiaircraft artillery fire.

"Enemy on the ground, two o'clock. They're running, jumping into a ditch. Guns," I yelled. Then I fired the gun.

"Rockets," Ruvalcaba said.

"Rockets," I repeated, and shot again.

When Ruvalcaba pulled off to the right, I kept shooting to the left until we were out of range of antiaircraft artillery. We made another pass, and I could still see the enemy on the ground, so Ruvalcaba fired more rockets. I could see bodies falling, but at first I couldn't tell if they were going down because they had been shot or because they were taking cover. The stillness below told me we killed them.

After taking out the enemy, Ruvalcaba returned the focus of our section to the battalion of armored personnel carriers.

Iraqi soldiers hiding in concealed positions could quickly re-man the armored carriers and attack the regiment with deadly fire. I was still in a state of high alert and ready to conduct more attacks.

Then the unthinkable happened. My .20 mm gun wouldn't fire. All the visualization in the world wasn't going to help me now. At the top of my display unit, which resembles a small TV, sits a heading tape that indicates flight direction and the direction the gun is pointing. The heading tape was spinning out of control and I couldn't target, let alone shoot at anything. Calmly, I relayed the problem to Ruvalcaba, and together we went through steps to get the weapons system back on line, but nothing worked.

"Sir, I can't do anything up here," I said.

I felt like a sitting duck. Just when it seemed like things couldn't get any worse, they did. Our wingman had run out of ammunition. Now both Cobras were sitting ducks. We needed to either find a way to fight back or get out of there.

There was one last way I might be able to employ the missiles. I quickly recoded my last three missiles, our wingman used his targeting system, and we started to shoot our missiles according to the other Cobra's laser. I said, "Missile away" and pressed the button. I heard the missile's rocket motor start up, and a few seconds later it was impacting the target. We targeted three more vehicles, both Cobras working in unison.

As we headed back to base, I realized how quickly I was breathing and exhaled slowly. Relief. The helicopters that left the fight earlier were sitting on the deck—safe, thank God. This was the first time the weapons systems had gone out on me while I was in the middle of an attack. Like I said, I was scared up there, but I didn't—wouldn't, couldn't—let my emotions exacerbate already tense circumstances. That could have lead to chaos, confusion, and a much more dangerous situation.

Everything I did during this crucial battle can be traced back to the training missions I had flown. I didn't get tunnel vision or become paralyzed by the problem, and neither did my fellow fighters. Instead, preparation and protocol allowed us to find a solution that kept us safe, on the offensive, and able to complete the mission with no casualties in the air or on the ground.

The systems we had to fall back on, the trust and knowledge we had in each other, and the ability to think fast and the agility to act faster was crucial to our success and survival. It all sure as hell kept me on the ball, not to mention breathing. That's why the plan is so important to the preparation. You can study and learn and practice, but if you don't have a formal backup system, you're in deep trouble. Systems keep you from giving in to uncertainty and disorder—they actually help to keep you calm and focused. I'm telling you, if Ruvalcaba and I hadn't been a strong team, with a set of protocols, you would not be reading this book. You gotta have a plan!

BACKWARD PLANNING SYSTEM (BPS)

Based on military strategy, Backward Planning Strategy, or BPS, is an excellent way to get unstuck if you're having trouble getting started. Prior to a raid in Iraq we would have nearly every move planned out backward, from (our desired) finish to start. You can see potential problems a little easier this way— you can't predict everything, but backward planning definitely brings to light considerations you may not have thought of had you just gone into a project headlong.

According to Marine philosophy, planning is a distinct process rather than a single act because it involves a number of ongoing and interdependent activities. Planning builds upon itself—each step should create a new understanding of the situation, which becomes the point of departure for new plans and goals.

The best backward planning encompasses two basic functions—visualizing a desired future and arranging actions in time and space that allow the vision to become real. Simply put, it's a way of figuring out how to move from your current situation to a more desirable situation.

BPS forces you to be very clear about the result you want. I've noticed that even in the corporate world, as well as in the entrepreneurial world, people can be fuzzy about the results they want, meaning the result they want to achieve is either too general or too unrealistic. By being clear about the result you want, you can be clear about how to achieve it.

NASA prepared for its Space Shuttle missions five years out, deciding who would be a mission specialist, who would do Petri dish experiments, and so on, so that they could create game plans for each of the individuals who would man or manage the tasks. In other words, NASA would envision precisely what they wanted a mission to look like and then go about creating the conditions to make it real. This is not the same thing as having an opinion about something (like the Earth is flat) and then going about proving it. It's about planning for an outcome (like I want to find out if the Earth is round or flat) and taking the correct steps to realize it (research other people's work in the area, take aerial photographs).

BPS can be useful in trying to meet any goal. I recently used it to train for a bodybuilding competition—once I got over my procrastination streak, I needed a definitive plan. I could schedule all the training sessions in the world, but if I didn't know what kind of body and skills I wanted to end up with, training wouldn't be effective or efficient.

My goal was simple and precise: I wanted to place in the contest. Not necessarily in the first position but definitely in the top twelve. What did I have to do to place? I had to weigh a certain amount, be able to lift a certain amount of weights, and learn to pose properly. That meant following a certain diet that would give me the right amount of lean protein and calories for energy and muscle building; working on my stamina and strength; and practicing poise, control, and balance. Now I could create an eating and workout regimen with my trainer. The actions were laid out in front of me; now all I had to do was take them on.

The Z2B exercise on page 78 describes how to do a BPS and challenges you to make one for yourself.

CRISIS PLANNING: DO IT; DON'T DWELL ON IT

I have to be honest: I revised this section at the last minute, as I watched oil pouring out of a busted pipe on the Gulf Coast on TV. It occurred to me that no one at British Petroleum (BP), who was running the rig, or the government disaster response agencies had done any advance "what if" planning because no one really seemed to have a plan—instead they spent valuable time trying to come up with a solution after the fact. Some say this was way too late.

During a press conference, White House Press Secretary Robert Gibbs made the understatement of the year when he said BP's disaster plan was insufficient to respond to the millions of gallons of oil spewing off the Gulf Coast. Gibbs stressed that companies need to have strong plans in place to respond to oil spills—before they happen.

One person asked Gibbs if the government, going forward, would require oil companies to have last-ditch switches on oil rigs to ensure that wells could be plugged. A blowout preventer failed to stop oil from gushing out of BP's oil well off the Gulf Coast, which led to the catastrophe. Other countries, such as Norway, require oil companies to have remote-control shut-off switches. The United States only *recommends* that oil companies use them. The BP well didn't have such a switch; having one might have been a very good element of crisis planning. Did BP execs, managers, and oil men ask themselves, "What's the worst that could happen" or "What if . . ." and then fill in the blank?

Tactical planning in the military, law enforcement, and even football training includes "what if" scenarios. The idea is that advance planning takes into account as many possible outcomes and potential problems, along with a response to each one. Clearly, some of the problems you imagine may never come to light, but it's better to be prepared than sorry. It's also true that some potential scenarios will send you back to the drawing board to retool your plans. Be thankful for that—uncovering a flaw in your strategy before implementation is better than finding out about it later, in the middle of executing it.

It's not a predictable world. Accidents, human error, and

wildly arbitrary events do happen. We can't always control or change circumstances, but we can expect the unexpected, plan for it, and manage our responses to it. There are two primary ways people make decisions, using either an analytical model or an intuitive model. Military leaders at all levels are very familiar with analytical planning because it is taught at military academies and we learn it during our formal training.

A Marine will prepare estimates of a situation using research, past tactical approaches, and as much current information about environment and conditions as possible. These estimates eventually become potential courses of action (or contingency plans). Analytical decision making uses a quantitative approach that includes research and near scientific accuracy. Whether you're embarking on a solo mission, like a long motorcycle ride through the Pacific Northwest, or working with a team on product development, you have to have three different kinds of plans in place:

1. *Master plan.* This is the best-case-scenario plan to get from point A to point B, Zero to Breakthrough. For example, the biker plans her trip when the weather is forecasted to be good; maps two routes—the most direct and an alternate; makes sure she has the correct provisions in the right quantities; gives key people her travel plans and contact information; and provides a list of days or times when she'll check in with them.

   The manager may brainstorm with her team on strategies for product development, manufacturing, pricing, rollout, and marketing and then provide the team with an action plan with defined roles and responsibilities.

2. *Contingency plan (or Plan B).* This is what you plan on doing if anything major goes wrong. What would be your response to the worst possible thing that could happen? For the biker, that may be getting in a bad accident, and she will need to determine what emergency steps she could and would take in that instance.

   The manager may have to establish responses to complete loss of funding; loss of key team members; or a disaster outside of her realm but directly affecting the shape of her business (such as a flood or a 9/11-style attack). In situations like these, you as leader have to take charge as well as inspire confidence in your team, encourage them, and take action.

3. *What if plan.* This is a plan or solutions to specific problems that may crop up during master plan execution. So, for instance, our motorcyclist may have contingency plans (including tools and supplies) for running out of gas unexpectedly; getting lost; bad weather like rain or extreme heat; unexpected road work and a detour; or a minor injury.

   The manager may assign different team members to handle particular situations that arise during the execution of plans. One person might be in charge of communication with stakeholders, including clearing up any miscommunications. Another might handle outside vendors and suppliers who are late in fulfilling their obligations or didn't follow instructions. The team leader could handle disciplinary actions and have a protocol in place before unacceptable behavior gets out of hand.

Ultimately, crisis planning is learning how to expect the unexpected and incorporate it into your strategy. If including contingency planning looks like it will take you longer to start on a goal or achieve it, so be it. It's not worth glossing over Murphy's Law (everything that can go wrong will go wrong) to make your journey shorter. On the other hand—and this is important—you can't dwell on the negative possibilities of every action. You have to be realistic and unemotional. If I had let myself dwell on the potential dangers of being a cop or flying a Cobra during a war, I still would be working as a trainer at a gym. Like I said earlier, seeing things for what they are, using common sense and planning, gives you confidence to deal with any problems that come up, whether they be in the sky, on the ground, in the classroom, or in the cubicle. Common sense may be one of the most overlooked and underused skills we've got going for us!

BREAK POINT CASE STUDY: FROM TRASH TO TREASURE

I was thinking about cleaning out my garage the other day, and like many necessary but very avoidable household tasks, my thoughts did not translate into action. With my speaking schedule, it's tough to find time to relax, let alone deal with clutter. I thought, wow, wouldn't it be great if someone would just come over and take some of this stuff off my hands so I wouldn't have to haul it away myself? Turns out somebody already thought of that idea—and it turned out to be an excellent one.

Even as a kid Brian Scudamore never liked clutter. His bed was made, his bookshelves were tidy, and his toys were neatly put away when not in use. Today, the same goes for his family. He told me that there's no junk in his house or his trunk (imagine that?). Ironically, he made junk his business, an idea based on his interest in entrepreneurship (he's had small businesses since he was a kid), love of neatness and order, and his desire to help other people.

The multimillion-dollar business he founded with a $700 investment in an old truck, 1-800-GOT-JUNK?, collects and distributes unwanted goods to recycling facilities in North American resale charity shops like the Salvation Army, and, when necessary, to landfills. What started as a small one-vehicle business in 1989 has become one of the fastest-growing franchises, with 325 locations in North America, a fleet of 1,000 trucks, and revenue of more than $107 million.

Who would have imagined such wild success—and big business—could be achieved by collecting other people's castoffs? Scudamore did—and it was all because he was trying to figure out a way to pay for college. Many years ago, while at McDonald's, he noticed a junk hauling truck in the drive-through line and inspiration struck. Somehow that image sparked an idea— to buy a box truck and offer to haul away people's extra and unwanted stuff for a flat fee. "When I get an idea, I take action whereas a lot of other people don't. There are those who have good ideas but they never make the connection to do something about them, and so they never take the next step," he told me.

He knew the one thing he needed to make the image real was a vehicle. He bought a used pickup and started advertising his services locally. Eventually, the service became so popular he had no time for college and dropped out. At that point Scudamore had three trucks and a handful of employees. It was then that he knew he had to create another plan—for the future success of the business.

The first thing he did was write out the specific result he wanted within five years: for the junk-hauling company to be in thirty U.S. and Canadian cities larger than Vancouver. "I imagined how we could engineer the future to get to the outcome we wanted. Step by step we made it happen. Because I look at a goal as pure potential, with no limits, and no insurmountable obstacles, reaching it is doable."

He changed the original name of the company, the Rubbish Boys, when an employee suggested "Got Junk?"—a takeoff on the "Got Milk?" campaign. Another lightning bolt: Scudamore knew the company name had to be 1-800-GOT-JUNK? He picked up the phone and called the number, and it rang an air traffic control office in Idaho. It was pure coincidence that the office's number spelled out GOT JUNK, so Scudamore called the office relentlessly asking if he could have the number. He continued to think backward from the result he wanted, and he knew that with a new name goes a new and identifiable logo. He did just that, and then tried out the design by painting a few of his trucks with it. Finally, the Idaho Department of Transportation gave him the number for free. Not only that, Scudamore hit his five-year goal sixteen days early.

His next result? To climb to $1 billion in total revenue and expand to two more countries. "With this company, I made the future happen in my mind first, and saw the successful results very clearly. Once I became very centered in that picture, I knew we would get there," he said. So what's the breakdown of Scudamore's success? This is what he did:

1. **Identified his passions:** Scudamore's were entrepreneurial businesses, order and neatness, and helping others.

2. **Acted on his lightbulb moment:** Scudamore found a simple way to bring these three things together when an idea struck as he saw a junk collector drive through a McDonald's—and then bought a truck, came up with a pricing structure, and started advertising his service locally.

3. **Filled a niche:** Scudamore realized that an organized, dedicated business, run professionally and dependably, could fill a niche and solve a problem many people have—too much stuff and no way to get rid of it all at once.

4. **Started small:** Scudamore developed a streamlined process for collecting and distributing the junk: flat-fee pickup on junk based on size of load, not hours it took to pack it; he had ready a list of organizations prepared to take the junk; and he coordinated pickups and drop-offs in the most efficient way possible.

5. **Visualized every step of the way:** Scudamore is a big believer in seeing results in the mind's eye. "I wrote out my painted picture in 1998, including what we would look like in five years, and we achieved every goal we set."

6. **Became a student of life:** "I question any leader in any area—you name it—people who have been successful

have had a clear vision, and there is a lot to learn from them," says Scudamore. There's always something new you can learn or an insight to be gained by listening.

7. **Built a financial model:** Scudamore's model was of a franchise system, thereby creating two revenue streams, junk collection and franchising.

8. **Envisioned a new result:** Scudamore set a new goal and created a plan for achieving it, and in the process grew the company.

BREAK POINT CASE STUDY: STRUMMING AWAY

One of the practices of great leaders and managers is that they never stop learning or seeking out new experiences in their professional lives but also—almost more important— in their personal lives. First of all, stretching your abilities or developing new ones gives you a connection to colleagues or employees who may be doing the same thing. You can relate to their struggles better, and in the process become a more dynamic and empathetic leader.

Combat Confidence: The Marine Corps uses the term "big blue arrow." It's a phrase that means "the general or basic plan." Whenever someone starts to explain a mission in too much depth and detail, someone else invariably stops them and says, "Just tell me the big blue arrow." If you're working with a team, remember to maintain their enthusiasm by letting them see the big picture, the basic strategy and the benefits, so they don't get bogged down with details they'll never remember.

Second, challenging yourself in an area that is completely separate from your daily life stretches your creative muscles and exercises the side of your brain you don't use as much at work. Ultimately, I believe this makes you a better problem solver. How often has the lightbulb gone off while you were riding a bike or playing Frisbee with your dog?

A friend of a friend of mine, Lisle, had a fairly high-stress job as a recruiter for a large company. It was her job to find good people to fill executive and management positions at the firm. She had always wanted to play the guitar. In fact, she bought a good acoustic guitar and kept it on a stand in the corner of her bedroom. She looked at it every morning when she got up and every evening when she went to sleep and invariably thought, "I'm going to learn to play that thing someday when I have time." Problem is, Lisle never had any time, or so she thought, because she was busy during the week with work and with sports and friends on the weekends.

One day a work colleague stopped by Lisle's apartment after an office volleyball game. She noticed the guitar and asked Lisle to play a tune for her. "I can't play it," Lisle said. "Why not? Why do you have it in your room if you can't use it?" the friend asked. "Well, I just haven't gotten around to learning," Lisle explained. "I can't seem to find the time, and I don't know where to start."

The friend suggested that Lisle pick a song that she liked and work on learning that. That way, she'd have a goal with a real-life outcome; instead of the goal being "learn to play the guitar," which seemed so *major*, or "learn to play chords," which seemed so general and, frankly, daunting, she'd have something to look forward to—a song. It didn't take Lisle that long to come up with her answer, because she always saw herself strumming Melissa Etheridge's "Come to My Window." "I want to be able to play that song when I have my first barbecue of the year," she said. That was only three months away. This was getting exciting!

Lisle had a guitar and she had a song—now all she needed was a teacher. Knowing that she wanted to learn to play a specific song in a specific genre meant she could go about finding the best teacher for her needs. If she had only the result in mind of "learning to play the strings of a guitar," she may have ended up with someone who taught classical music or was into a style of teaching that concentrated on chords and repetition. This way she was able to talk to teachers and interview them about their techniques and her needs. She found a teacher who specialized in teaching guitar through specific songs—and the teacher was also a folk guitarist on the side. Perfect!

Not only that, but Lisle was honest about her time commitment—she could take a two-hour lesson once a week and devote sixty minutes to practice five days a week, with a little more on the weekend. She enlisted her friend and colleague to act as her Breakthrough Buddy (BTB) to support the effort by sending weekly e-mail reminders and encouragement.

Funny thing is, this way of studying guitar worked well for Lisle, because while she was learning to play a tune she liked, she also learned all the basics to get there—strumming, chords, positioning, tuning, and playing notes. By the end of eight weeks, she could play the tune fairly well—at the end of the third month she was ready for her debut at her backyard party. And by working on that one song, she learned enough to read and play the notes of other tunes. Since Lisle focused on playing songs she liked, she kept up her playing and practicing and over time built up a large repertoire.

Lisle also received a professional bonus from learning to play the guitar. First, achieving a skill so different from those used in her job gave her a chance to free her mind from her job. Guitar playing required absolute focus—it didn't work if she let the thoughts of the day interfere in her lessons and practice. Second, mastering a tune gave her a renewed sense of confidence at work—a nice overflow effect. "I'm less reticent about asking a manager to be more specific about what he or she wants," she says. Another bonus? Playing the guitar has become a great way to unwind after a hard day at work.

Here's why Lisle finally was able to learn how to play the guitar:

1. **Got specific:** She took her friend's advice and determined what outcome she wanted—to play a specific song for a specific occasion. She realized her procrastination was caused by giving herself too big a task, "learning to play the guitar," as opposed to something more manageable and enjoyable, "learning to play a favorite song."

2. **Found the right teacher:** Lisle's instructor specialized in teaching guitar through tune learning.

3. **Enlisted a BTB:** Lisle asked a friend to be on "standby" to support her goal—she committed to being available for weekly check-ins by e-mail or telephone.

4. **Focused on a short-term goal:** Setting a goal to learn one song in three months and expanding the goal only after meeting the first small one made it achievable.

Z2B EXERCISE: BACKWARD PLANNING, STEP BY STEP (BPS)

The best-laid plans always start at the end. Backward planners know how to eliminate everything that doesn't support the result they want because BPS allows you to see more of the big picture, flaws and all. The hard part may be in choosing the result—is it a long-term goal or a short-term achievement? How about both? BPS can be used for making a three-course dinner, plotting out a new business, or winning a war. For the sake of this exercise, especially if this is the first time you have done a backward plan, choose something relatively short-term to work with, as I did with the bodybuilding competition.

This is by no means a universal planning or tactical technique appropriate for all endeavors—there really isn't one. BPS is just a way of getting started, to jump-start your thinking and to define the result you want. Always adapt your planning methods to the particulars of your situation. In my experience holding workshops in the corporate and public sectors and talking to large organizations, I've seen an inclination to overinstitutionalize planning methods.

That inflexibility often leads to "lockstep thinking." No one wants to upset the apple cart when that's exactly what they should be doing—it's the only way fresh ideas get put out in the open. Instead, smart people from all levels of the company with good ideas may be afraid to bring them up for fear of looking like an outsider or going against the grain. That's a shame. Sure, planning takes discipline, but taking it to the extreme means missing out on contrary points of view that just may hold the key to the door you want to unlock.

1. *Write down the result you want.* Putting a goal or objective down on paper firms it up and makes it real. Seeing is believing.

2. *Identify the final step to your goal.* Going from the result, what is the accomplishment you would need to make just before reaching your goal? Write it down under the result. For mine—placing in the top twelve of a bodybuilding competition—it would be to go through the required rounds of competition successfully. So how do I get there?

3. *List the activities it takes to accomplish your goal.* For me it was weight training, eating properly, practicing, and learning as much as I could about other potential competitors. Some activities can be done simultaneously, while others have to be done in sequence. The only way you can figure out which is which is to write everything down and start playing with it.

4. *Eliminate the extraneous.* Is there anything on the list that doesn't seem necessary? Are you performing routine tasks that aren't really getting you closer to your goal or preventing you from achieving it? Get rid of them and leave only those activities that support your mission. For me, it was cutting down on aerobic exercise and increasing weight-bearing routines—less time on the treadmill and more time on the bench press. As for my diet, an appointment with a sports nutritionist helped me pinpoint foods I was eating that were hindering my progress and identify others that I should be putting on my plate.

5. *Identify potential problems.* Here's your chance to see holes in your plan, revise, build in flexibility, and do some contingency planning. If this step takes a little

time, so be it. It's worth the extra energy to make sure you've looked at your goal from every angle and addressed eventualities. I made a "make-up" schedule in case I missed a training session, a definite possibility with my schedule. I also took a hard look at my timeline and made adjustments to build in a buffer of a week or two in case I got sick.

6. *Prioritize.* Okay, so now that you have a backward plan, you can flip it. Which steps do you need to take first? Which ones must be done simultaneously? In other words, are all your steps in the right order? Use the Pareto principle (Vilfredo Pareto was a nineteenth-century Italian economist) or the 80/20 rule: 80 percent of our activities produce 20 percent of the results, while only 20 percent of our activities produce 80 percent of the results. List the top ten priorities in order of value, and concentrate on the first two. The other eight will fall into place organically.

7. *Make a timeline.* How much time will each activity take before you can move on to the next one or reach your goal? Be realistic. A given task might take a few hours to complete (research, for example), but do you have three consecutive hours to devote to it or will you need to break up those hours over a few days? Maybe you can lose ten pounds in a month, but is that really wise, and are you in fact going to be able to do it? Maybe give yourself two months. Work and the time it takes to do it are parts of a whole. Going through time estimates also lets you see exactly where you are

wasting time—I found several time slots in the day where I could fit in a training session, time that was being underused by unimportant tasks or tasks that could easily be delegated.

8. *Mark to-dos on the calendar, and then do them.* Don't simply make a to-do list; schedule tasks (Monday: phone calls and follow-up e-mails; Tuesday: work on marketing; Wednesday: budget planning; and so on). When you make appointments and put them in your datebook or BlackBerry, you tend to keep them. You'll also avoid "double booking" yourself or completely forgetting! Putting things in writing is powerful. Seeing activities correlated with dates on a calendar also helps you see how time is allocated—are you really giving yourself enough of it to finish certain jobs? Can you build in a buffer on the front or back end of an activity to compensate for unforeseeable events?

9. *Gather your crew; ask a wingman or BTB for feedback.* Another set of eyes can often point out something critical you may have overlooked, contribute helpful ideas, or sharpen your strategy.

10. *Verify before implementing.* Have you ever planned an evening out at a restaurant, and then gotten there only to find it's closed on Wednesday nights? What about making a trip to a specialty store—only to arrive and find an abandoned building with a FOR RENT sign dangling from the front door? Hate that! That's why I always call first, before I get in my truck and head

out. Same thing with a plan—if you are depending on any outside resources, check to make sure they are available. If not, make the necessary alterations. And congratulate yourself for saving valuable time and money.

ALL IN A DAY'S WORK

I hope you're beginning to see how the strategies in Zero to Breakthrough build on one another. Finding your passion gives you a direction, research tells you what you know and don't know, planning helps to reveal and foresee potential challenges and problems before they happen, and knowledge allows you to find solutions so you can be flexible and responsive (Chapter 3) and confront obstacles (Chapter 4).

If you think about it, when you're planning and preparing for a goal, you are actually mastering a large part of what you've set out to accomplish. That's pretty cool. And laying all that groundwork puts you in the driver's seat—and not at the mercy of outward forces, distractions, and surprises. This is where intellectual capital converges with action. By basing our thoughts on research and study and projecting them forward in time to influence events *before* they occur rather than merely responding to them *as* they occur, we prepare ourselves for anything.

The Marines call the result of such planning "command and control." In order to be successful at command and control, the execution of your plan, you have to have discipline. The next chapter is all about supple execution and focused action.

FLY-AWAYS

- Accept failure as the food for the seeds of success.

- You can discard procrastination as an excuse.

- There is no bliss where there is ignorance.

- The best-laid plans start with research, knowledge, and understanding.

- Realistic planning reduces confusion and danger.

- Backward planning is the most efficient way to start on and reach a goal.

- Include worst-case scenarios in every plan, but don't let the thought of them paralyze you.

CHAPTER 3

Sit Up and Go!
Discipline and Execution

Victory belongs to the most perservering.

—NAPOLEON BONAPARTE

Two flights are forever etched in my mind—firsts both—
and each emphasize the importance of planning and procedure to achieving breakthroughs. It was an awesome day
when I took my first solo flight after training for months—
the sun was high; azure blue skies punctuated by puffy white
clouds provided a stunning background for the mountains in
the distance. A slight breeze cooled the air. I checked out my
flight gear, flight vest, and helmet. I grabbed my flight bag and
headed out to the airfield. As I walked toward my chariot, I
trembled slightly, not from fear but from excitement and pride.

I had studied and flew and studied and flew to ready myself
for this moment. If you can imagine taking a test every day in

school, that's what flight school and training were like. Every time I flew, I was being evaluated, judged, and graded. I prepared for each brief and flight as if my life depended on it—because I knew that someday it would.

And now, here I was, about to take my first solo trip—not a lesson, not a class, not a practice. Once I had geared up and was in the air, I thought, "Oh, I can go through my takeoff checklist faster," and so I scanned my kneeboard, felt confident everything was A-OK, and pulled out of my parking spot. Once in the air, I was feeling pretty cool.

Then I noticed that everything in and outside the aircraft seemed too peaceful. After realizing there was no radio call and my compass had gone down, I looked frantically around at my controls. I grabbed the kneeboard to go over emergency procedures for lost communications. I checked and rechecked but could not see one thing on the list that I had skipped. After moving the kneeboard I looked down at my switches and controls and realized that the actual kneeboard had landed right on the master switch when it fell to the side, turning everything off. I flipped the switch back on, and just at that moment, the air controller was trying to reach me at the flight checkpoint! Even though I hadn't skipped anything, it was then that I understood how important even the seemingly most trivial detail is to the disciplined—and safe—execution of plans.

Flash forward to my first flight in a combat zone. My journey to that point had been an arduous, demanding, frustrating one, and sometimes—I'll admit it—a roller coaster. When I was going through Naval flight school, I wanted to fly jets. When I was assigned to helicopter training, I knew I wanted to fly the baddest copter out there—the Cobra. That was one of the first modifications I made to my plans as a Marine, a modification that was imposed on me by not making the cut for fighter jet. That was okay—instead of throwing in the towel, I just went after an aircraft that, as it turned out, suited me well. When a Marine aviator is at its controls, it's the fiercest fighting machine there is. Had I not been willing to adapt the execution of my plans to be a flying Marine, I might never have found that out.

During flight school and practice runs, pilots learn the procedures and tasks that make up thorough preflight check and efficient "cockpit management." Strategy can't be implemented, let alone modified as situations change without procedures that essentially free you to carry out and change plans when necessary.

The Marines, like many other well-oiled organizations, make a clear distinction between planning and procedure. Planning for particular actions stops with execution, and even then adaptation continues during execution. So knowing and following through on tasks, even though some seemed repetitive or mundane, was essential. How can you execute a well-thought-out plan if you aren't willing to complete its steps?

Pilots have to be efficient with their set-up and use of the cockpit so they can access what they need when they need it. We can't spend twenty minutes looking for a map. The routine went something like this: I put a lumbar cushion on my seat, which helped reduce back pain, scooted me closer to the cyclic stick (used for turning the aircraft left and right), and allowed me to comfortably rest my arm on my thigh.

Next, I stored my gas mask and night vision goggles (NVGs) behind my left shoulder and stored my emergency procedures book behind my left elbow. I removed a cushion from where my left arm would rest and replaced it with maps. I placed my NVG mount on top of the dash. Extra batteries got tucked into the cracks of the padding on my right. On the inside of my seat armor behind my right elbow was an inverted M-4 (a smaller version of the M-16 rifle). A Camelback water container hung over the side of the seat.

After I completed setting up the cockpit, I climbed into the front seat, as I had practiced many times. From this station, you work a majority of the weapon systems and navigate while in transit. I put on my helmet and strapped in, clasping the five-point seat harness and making sure it was locked. The Cobra typically carries missiles, rockets, and guns; no passengers on this baby. The front or gunners' seat, which is where I was had flown 90 percent of my initial flights, was primarily for operating the weapons systems. This is a critical task because it calls on the pilot to identify if an image is an enemy or not. As a new pilot, this could be seen as a very daunting task and is why there is such an intense focus on studying and recognition.

Less than a year before this flight, I was driving to base when I heard a radio report about a plane hitting the Pentagon. I left home that morning after witnessing live news reports of two planes striking the World Trade Center. As I drove up to the front gate, I expected it to be locked down tight, but they were waving cars through as usual. I parked and ran inside the building. As expected, the TV was on in the Ready Room and my fellow pilots were staring at the screen in disbelief. There was no flying on that day or for several days to come.

The next time I strapped into my Cobra, it took on a different meaning. I wasn't just being tested; I was preparing for the flight of my life. I knew few things for sure about the days ahead, but I certainly wasn't going to take a procedure, process, or step for granted. My kneeboard would be treated with respect. I would no longer look at repetitive tasks as humdrum or trivial. There was a lot more at stake now than my commander's approval. A few short months later, I found myself in Kuwait, waiting to take that test—the start of the Iraq War.

THE ART OF DOING

> **Combat Confidence:** There are only two ways to succeed: the first time, and again.

Discipline. Even the sound of the word seems harsh, final. What do you think of when you hear the word? A stern teacher tapping a ruler on her desk? Sitting in a corner for a time-out? Yeah, I know, I never looked forward to detention, loss of privileges, or curfews, either. But that's kid's stuff. "Punishment" is only one meaning of the word. Here are a few others: order and control; training to ensure proper behavior; calm, controlled behavior; conscious control over lifestyle; restraint. Under those definitions, discipline is actually very liberating. Once you have control over yourself, you can pretty much determine your own fate. If you give in to bad habits or lazy tendencies, well, you're at their mercy. Discipline saves you from that. Of course, you have to work at it—it is discipline, after all.

For Marines (as well as cops, firefighters, football players, and many others), discipline is an essential part of "mission accomplishment." When General Charles C. Krulak became the thirty-first Commandant of the Marine Corps in 1995, he refocused the Marine Corps on its core values—honor, courage, and commitment; and discipline is integral to all of these. In fact, it's one of the main reasons that the Marine Corps has endured as one of the country's institutions of excellence.

It takes consistent discipline to execute plans. It's worth noting that the Marines in particular draw distinctions among a plan (your route to a goal or destination), a process (a dynamic system of related activities, or details, that achieve a specific outcome), and a procedure (a prescribed sequence of steps for accomplishing a specific task). Execution of plans requires both process and procedure. Details and discipline keep you honest. As a pilot, for instance, ignoring a pre-flight checklist could mean a literal crash landing, putting comrades in danger, or just generally failing to complete a mission. As a cop, neglecting procedures could mean allowing a perpetrator to "walk" on a technicality or missing an important factor in an investigation.

When I started training for the Marines, I went down to Pensacola, Florida, for flight school. Every Marine Corps aviator is a naval aviator because there is no Marine Corps Flight School (the Corps is part of the Department of the Navy). They call it Pensacola Wings of Gold. You go through a six-week period of Aviation Pre-Flight Indoctrination (API), and it's during those six weeks that you're tested on swimming.

Before I started, I went to a Marine swim house (where we could practice our swim test) and approached an instructor to ask if he could show me how to do the swim. "Look, swimming is a weakness of mine," I told him. "I know how to swim and I can float; I can survive a little splashing and jumping off the diving board and stuff like that. But the formal stroke-breath thing, I need some help with that."

The instructor said, "Ma'am, show up here Monday morning and we will get you squared away." He seemed confident, so I figured I could show a little buoyancy, too (pun intended!). Two weeks before school started, I showed up at the pool house and immediately was ordered to jump in the pool. I worked with the teachers one on one and swam by myself three or four times a week, in my uniform, to simulate the test. The instructor taught me what's commonly called the dead man's float.

"Ma'am, get in the water, just let your head dangle in the water, let your arms dangle, let your feet dangle, and take a deep breath before you put your head in. Bend your head up, breathe, put your head in the water, and blow out."

They were starting me out easy. I got the hang of it in about ten seconds.

"All right, next we are going to tread water." Do you know how to tread water? Is it as hard for you as it was for me? Two instructors got on their haunches and explained the method to me: "Ma'am, put your arms here and do this with them," said one, moving his limbs horizontally in the air. The other guy then told me to move my legs in a circular fashion (at least I didn't have to chew gum and talk at the same time!). "Don't stiffen your legs," he said, "keep 'em moving." I was going to say "Marco" and I knew that somebody was going to say "Polo" back. Right?

Finally I got my arms and legs coordinated and moving in sync. I was about half an inch above the water line so I could breathe (I knew enough about swimming to know that if you let your head go under you'll panic and it will be very difficult to rescue you). I was thinking, this is great . . . until I heard one of the teachers say, "Ma'am, you can't do that." Huh? Do what? "No," I say, "I *am* doing it, I'm treading."

"No, you're not," he said, "you're swimming backward."

I said, "I am going to be in the middle of the ocean, who is going to see me?" Water survival, right? Wrong!

The instructors were trying to teach me the most effi-cient way to conserve energy and survive if something should happen to me and I were to go down over the middle of the ocean. Okay, I got it. I went to the pool every day until I could tread water with the best of them—and the teachers continued to show me everything that I needed to know. When school started up, there was a six-week course in API. At the end of week five, I had to do the one-mile swim in my flight suit. Everyone in the class was given the standard safety brief. It was a Friday morning, so we'd have the weekend off to relax, recharge, hang out, and do our thing.

Even though I had trained, I was not looking forward to

the test, not even a little bit. I had a good foundation, but here's the deal: Marine pilots have to be able to swim one mile in their flight suit in less than eighty minutes. You can't touch the ground, you can't touch the buoys, you can't touch anything. You are alone in that swimming pool—just as you would be had your helicopter gone down over water. One mile. In a flight suit. Have you seen a flight suit? Not exactly Victoria's Secret material.

"Okay!" said the instructor, "breathe, and jump in the water." Everybody bolted up from their seats and dove in. I was still sitting there looking at the ground, petrified. *If I don't make this swim, I don't become a pilot. I have to do it all over again.*

And the instructor walked over to me and said, "Ma'am, you're going to be okay. You've got to do this."

"Are you sure?"

"Go get in the water," he said.

I got up and slowly walked to the edge of the pool. After all, I had to conserve energy. Once I was in the water, the start whistle blew and everybody took off. I was swimming my little heart out, going as fast as I could. About twenty minutes into it, I heard one of the instructors say, "Come on, ma'am, pick it up, you have to go faster, if you don't you are not going to make it. Come on, pick it up, you've got to go faster."

Now, have you ever been doing something the best you can, working your hardest, and it's still not good enough—and someone is letting you know it? That's how I felt right then, and I wanted to scream at the top of my lungs, "I'm *trying.*" All these feet were passing me by left and right, kicking and splashing, just feet everywhere. I thought, "I have to do something, and I have to do it now. Those feet that are passing me right now, I am not going to let them get more than twelve inches from the front of my face."

Have you ever been around a lot of folks when you were going through something difficult? If you don't feel that they understand, it can make you feel "alone in the crowd." That's how I felt, up to my neck in water, with limbs and goggles moving all around me. So with laser-sharp intensity and focus, I came up, took a breath, and went. Up breathe, down feet. That rhythm kept me going for a good while.

Then, all of the sudden, I started seeing fewer feet and arms. Wow, wait a minute—the others were done with their mile, and I was still swimming. So I started moving at what I thought was a faster pace. I was mistaken: I heard the disembodied voices of the instructors, standing somewhere on the deck above me say, "Come on, ma'am, you've got to pick it up. You aren't going to make it, you're going to have to pick it up." During the last couple of laps, I didn't hear any voices.

As I climbed up the ladder and out of the pool I asked, "Did I make it?"

Combat Confidence: What do successful people do? These four things:
1. Don't make excuses.
2. Commit to their commitment.
3. Take action no matter how minor it may seem.
4. Review, recharge, and reattack.

"Ma'am, you did it in seventy-two minutes." Whew. I was good. I didn't have to do it again. Mission accomplished.

Make no mistake, if I had not made the mile in time, I would have done it again—no question about it. I didn't want to do it again, but not making it the first time would not have been a signal to quit for me. And it didn't matter one whit to me that I was the last one out of the pool. Discipline is sticking with a thing so you can finish it. It gives you the power to execute beyond what you think is the best of your ability. Discipline lets you push your own envelope.

FAILURE IS A PUSH IN THE RIGHT DIRECTION (BUT ONLY IF YOU CAN READ THE SIGNS)

I talk a lot about failure in Zero to Breakthrough, one, because it's applicable to almost every situation in life, and two, because it's one of the most important tools for developing a breakthrough mentality. Unfortunately, perfection is reserved for God. Even the most prepared among us can come in last in a race, falter at a test, or blow a presentation. That's why we all have to put failures to work for us, not against us. Failures tell us what we don't know and what we need to work on. Oh, yeah, and they do build character, if you're willing to eat some humble pie, own up to it, and try again. Failure is not your final destination.

I joined my Marine squadron on July 29, 2001. A few months later, I remember going through the front gate of Camp Pendleton and hearing about the Twin Towers. By February 12, 2003, I found myself, boots on the ground, in Kuwait getting ready to cross the border and go into Iraq. About four or five months down the line, after President Bush declared the war officially over, they decided they were going to give everyone in my squadron a tactics test. I was thinking, hmm, I haven't really been studying a whole lot. Where did that discipline that I had with me in the swimming pool go?

I gathered up my tactical manual, safety manual, and any other manual I had on hand and took them with me on a four-day mission into Iraq. I figured I could get a lot of studying done. I came back the next day to take the test, feeling as if I had reviewed what I could, and studied as much as possible. Fifteen minutes into the test I said to myself, "I'm not doing so hot." The next day confirmed what I had dreaded: I had bombed. Bombed.

And it was hard, very hard to own. It was devastating, actually.

Failing the tactics test was a blow on so many levels. This was another obstacle I created for myself because I had not been studying as I was supposed to. I had let myself down, yes, but I also felt I had let down women, minorities, the military, and perhaps most important, the guys in my squadron. I was afraid that my failure would keep them from seeing the full potential of any woman or minority. The lead tactics instructor asked me why I had not asked my peers about what would be on the test because he had given them the information that would be on the test. I didn't have an excuse, and it didn't really matter— ultimately I was accountable for the knowledge, whether my buddies had the information or not. The question was: What was I going to do about it? Take the test again, of course.

I went back to the books, and the next week I took the test over and passed it with flying colors. Everything was fine, but the initial failure still hurt. It took a while for me to get rid of that ache. Now, how many times have you failed a test? Maybe we're sore at ourselves, our heads are hung in shame, maybe we're on probation. One semester I had a 1.0 average in college. I never really talked about that before I started public speaking. But I'm still here; we're all still here.

Sometimes you have to suit up and go more than once. One more time: Failure is not a destination; it's just fuel for the road.

BLOOM WHERE YOU'RE PLANTED

The Marine Corps likes to move its people around to give everyone a well-rounded experience and appreciation for the organization. Different jobs prepare you for advancement as well—you can't get ahead if you stay in the stockroom. At one point the higher-ups decided to move me to Headquarters Marine Corps in Quantico, Virginia. I asked for orders to be placed in the recruiting office, and my orders officer at the time agreed.

I felt this was a perfect spot for me—I was enthusiastic about the Corps, and I was determined to get the image of a minority woman in a flight suit out to college students, especially women and minorities. I was in college when I saw that woman, and her image is the reason I am here today. The Marines had given me so much, and I wanted to spread the news.

Two weeks before I was supposed to leave, I was told there had been a change of orders.

"Captain Armour, you aren't going to recruiting," the officer told me. "You're going to Equal Opportunity."

"What? Just because I am a black chick, I have to work in E. O.? How equal is that?" I thought. I was pissed.

Have you ever heard the expression, "Bloom where you're planted"? It's when you end up somewhere you didn't intend or imagine, and you might not even think you'll like it, but you make the best of it and do a darn good job. You even end up flourishing. Your reputation and your integrity are on the line: The job you do is a reflection on you. The other half of it is that it's more productive to be happy or at least positive than it is to be resentful and discontented, especially when circumstances are temporarily out of your control. Your reaction to those circumstances is *always* under your control.

I wasn't so much disappointed with the new assignment as I was frustrated that I wouldn't have a chance to recruit. I decided to give it a try (actually, I had no choice: orders are orders) and make the best of it. I took to the job right away, and in retrospect it was a good fit for me. I learned a lot about the meaning of diversity and what it can do for a team or an organization. Diversity is not just about having a mix of ethnicities and genders; it's about bringing together a range of ideas and outlooks. I talk more about the value of diversity later, but suffice it to say that you have to be willing to suit up and go when duty calls, even if the assignment is not your first choice. Execute to the best of your ability—not doing so or stubbornly refusing to go where they send you is a kind of self-imposed failure before even trying.

DID YOU KNOW HELICOPTERS CAN FLY BACKWARD? AGILE IMPLEMENTATION

On my second day on the job as a cop—I was only twenty-three at the time—I was in the car with my buddy Matt. It was my first time driving the cruiser, and we were getting ready to do a routine traffic stop. I had the wheel at ten and two.

Matt said, "Okay, see that truck? We're going to pull it over for excessive fumes. Turn on the lights."

"Oh, yeah," I said, "they're going to get a huge ticket—look at all those fumes coming out!"

"Look at that," Matt said almost as soon as the lights went on, "they're taking off—take off after them!"

A pursuit? *"Go!"*

From there our conversation went something like this:

Me: "Do I turn on the sirens?"
Matt: "Turn on the sirens!"
Me: "They are turning right!"
Matt: "Turn right."
Me: "They're turning in to the projects."
Matt: "Turn in to the projects."
Me: "They hit the Dumpster!"
Matt: "Don't hit the Dumpster!"

The passenger and driver bailed, and Matt said, "I have the driver, you get the passenger."

I got out and started running . . . and tripped over a crack in the sidewalk. How embarrassing. Thank God it was two o'clock in the morning and people weren't up yet.

So the passenger, a woman, started running hard and fast. I yelled, "Stop, police, get on the ground! Stop, police, get on the ground!" but this woman had no intention of slowing down. The "perp" was nearly six feet tall and weighed about ninety-five pounds, so she could really fly. Have you ever been running so fast that you felt as if flames were coming out of your chest? That's how I felt. I wasn't so cocky anymore. This was a big reality check.

The woman cut around a corner, and I followed as fast as I could, all the while thinking, "If this woman doesn't stop, she's going to get away from me." By this time people in their apartments had been roused by the noise and were looking out their windows. And I looked up at everybody looking at me. The passenger "fugitive" looked back and saw me still chasing her. As suddenly as she started running from the truck she stopped, got on the ground, and dropped into a spread-eagle position. I ran up to her and asked, "Why were you running?" Thinking in my head, "Thank God she stopped." She looked at me and said, "I was scared."

"You don't run from the police, ma'am." I stood there a moment longer and caught my breath, then knelt down and cuffed her, got her up, and said, "Come on."

What did I learn from the execution of my first pursuit? You don't stand up, dust the donut crumbs off your shirt, and check out the hole in your brand-new trousers! You take off with 100 percent force and commitment. That's the breakthrough mentality. It takes confidence and discipline to take off from where you are. I was able to follow the procedures and rules of pursuit automatically; as a result the chase was successful *despite* the fact that it was a total surprise to me that the woman took off like greased lightning.

When you start working toward your goal, as the plan unfolds, things may not, well, always go according to plan. Do they ever? That's why you follow the contingency and "what if" planning outlined in Chapter 2. Too bad that even carefully laid-out responses to various scenarios may not pan out, either. Things you didn't predict may happen. What then? New contingencies may have to be implemented at a moment's notice. Sometimes— like when you're being shot at—you don't have time to pick and choose your responses. You have to act in the moment.

The ability to reassess your steps, continue to develop your plan, and change direction midstream isn't a one-two-three, easy proposition. Our instincts usually tell us to take the path of least resistance, but this often isn't the same road that leads us from Zero to Breakthrough. Reassessing plans midstream certainly does not come naturally for most of us; it didn't for me. One of my greatest and most useful achievements has been learning how to sense when something is about to change, and then adapting to it in advance by shifting what I'm doing in midstream.

GO WITH YOUR GUT

Over the course of time, especially while in the military, I've developed the ability to trust my instincts—and act on them. There have been so many times when I could honestly feel a shift in the energy of a situation and I'd know a change was coming. You see, when you're up in the air and the enemy comes out of nowhere and starts shooting at you, the analytical method of planning doesn't really help you much. Intuition and agility are all you've got, and you'd better use them because there's no time for data collection and brainstorming sessions. Once you're engaged with the enemy (or a fellow competitor or any new set of circumstances), you can't afford the time it would take to review the situation and revise your plans. There's no time for excuses, either—it's all about results.

Intuitive decision making relies on something called qualitative assessment: making instantaneous decisions using the full force of your experience, knowledge, and intuition. Temperament and personality can impact an individual's intuitive skills for better or worse (coming from a military family must have something to do with my ability to focus and decide when under stress), but they can also be nurtured and strengthened with practice and experience. The more experience you have, the more confidence you have in your intuition, and the more successful your snap decisions will be. In time-sensitive situations, intuitive decision making is not about finding the ideal solution; it's about finding the one that's going to work *right now*.

The Marines call this OODA: Observe-Orient-Decide-Act, a process used when one is faced with a situation that demands an immediate reaction. Colonel John R. Boyd, U.S. Air Force (Retired), observed this phenomenon and formalized it into the concept of OODA, and the concept was incorporated into Marine doctrine in 1989. OODA is nothing new, but it wasn't codified in this way until fairly recently, at least as it relates to the history of warfare strategy. Sun Tzu noted in the classic *Art of War* that "speed is the essence of war." Napoleon believed that the intuitive ability to assess a battlefield situation and make a sound decision quickly was a commander's most valuable skill. General Patton also knew that "a good plan executed now is better than a perfect plan executed next week."

There are so many examples of battles lost because a leader

failed to make a timely decision—any decision—as opposed to making a bad one quickly. The longer you delay decision in a time-sensitive situation, the more opportunities you miss to adapt or correct. Inaction also can fortify the enemy, or the "other guy," depending on the situation, by allowing him to take advantage of the time your indecision leaves. OODA is both offensive and defensive—it can interfere with an opponent's decision-making process and greatly reduce his ability to impose his will. Beautiful, right?

OODA doesn't only apply on the battlefield. Anyone can use OODA to make consistently faster and better decisions. One of the most dramatic and impressive examples of OODA outside of the military was at the 1950 Monaco Grand Prix. If you are at all into racing, you probably know this story. The great Argentine race-car driver Juan Manuel Fangio rocketed out from the front-row starting slot and took the lead on the first lap. On his second lap, Fangio burst out of the tunnel into the sunlight and glanced up at what he thought would be an adoring crowd overlooking the quay.

He noticed something odd: They weren't looking at him—they were looking *away* from him. He remembered looking through a photo album at the Monaco Auto Club the day before. Pictures of a 1936 race came to mind; it showed cars that had skidded and crashed on the same quay he was approaching at 100 miles per hour. In a matter of seconds, Fangio Observed, Oriented, Decided, and Acted: He broke hard to a stop before the left turn.

Around that bend, hidden from his view by a balustrade, were nine crashed Grand Prix cars. During the first lap, another driver, Nino Farina, had skidded. Eight cars behind him had crashed into him and, naturally, into each other. Luckily there were no serious injuries. The road was blocked, but Fangio again saw his only chance: If just one car could move over, he could get by it and keep going. He managed to get close enough to a car and actually pushed its tire with his hand and rolled it far enough away for him to pass. From there he went on to a victorious finish. Keep in mind all of this happened in a matter of minutes, if not seconds. In Fangio's case, experience and knowledge of racing enabled him to sense a change, make a series of quick decisions, modify his racing strategy, and come out the winner.

Since we're talking about winning, let's talk about football! I love football—watching and playing it. In fact, I was a running back for the San Diego Sunfire women's professional football team for a while. So as you can imagine, Super Bowl Sunday is a day I look forward to, not for the wings and commercials but for the actual game. The 2009 Super Bowl is a perfect example of what happens when you don't use your intuitive skills to make decisions and take action. It's what happens when you lose focus and underestimate the other guy.

This game made the record books for the longest play in Super Bowl history—a hundred-yard interception return for a touchdown by the Pittsburgh Steelers' linebacker James Harrison. For more than three quarters of the game, the Steelers were heading toward victory. Then the Arizona Cardinals scored 16 points in the fourth quarter. With just thirty-five seconds left in the game, the Cardinals lost their composure and didn't use their instincts that were telling them (or should have been telling them) not to underestimate their opponent.

The Steelers used that crack in the other team's facade, that hesitation to act, with one monstrous, improbable play: a six-yard touchdown pass that resulted in a soaring 27 to 23 victory. Always keep your cool and never give your rival the benefit of the doubt because anything can—and usually does—happen.

BECOMING A QUICK-THINKING, DECISIVE ACTOR IN THE THEATER OF LIFE (OR WAR)

It's impossible to prepare yourself for every single situation you'll be placed in. No one can say for sure where his or her Zero to Breakthrough journey is going to lead—and what external events are going to occur along the way. Did anyone getting on a subway car in Manhattan on the morning of September 11, 2001, know that buildings would be falling down as they pulled into their stop? How can you prepare for that? It used to be unthinkable; now, of course, it's not.

The best way to prepare for any eventuality, including decisions or actions that are ethical in nature, is to have consistent values—a moral compass, if you will. The Marines call it sound character, and having sound character puts you in a position of making better judgments more often than not. What are your values? You have to know them before you can apply them to decision making and the execution of plans. How you implement your plans is actually more important than what your plans are. If you cheat, take shortcuts when they aren't appropriate, or lower your standards just to get something done, you're not achieving breakthrough.

Decisions and actions based on your personal principles should be a habit, something done naturally. The three I like come from the Marines (of course): honor, courage, and commitment. Take any plan or activity—let's use my body-building competition:

1. *Honor.* In working toward my goal I plan to honor and respect the rules of the competition; likewise I will honor the promise to my trainer and to myself that I will be consistent and steady.

2. *Courage.* I will have the courage to continue to train and compete, even if my confidence gets shaky or the competition looks stiff. I will have the courage to accept the outcome of my efforts.

3. *Commitment.* I will stand by my commitment to train even if I'm sore, tired, and cranky, and would rather go to a friend's barbecue than spend Saturday in the gym.

> **Combat Confidence:** Integrity, courage, initiative, decisiveness, mental agility, and personal accountability are the basic skills you need to act quickly, decisively, accurately, and ethically.

RULES OF ENGAGEMENT

Great decision making, commitment to a mission, and discipline are best achieved when you are personally engaged in the task at hand. I'll go out on a limb and say that if you like, understand, and believe in what you're doing, it's very easy to commit to doing it well. A lot of undisciplined, sloppy work comes from the people who are the least engaged in their jobs. A 2009 Global Workforce Study by Towers Perrin, an HR consultancy, polled more than 90,000 workers and found something startling: Barely one in five employees (21 percent) is fully engaged on the job.

Eight percent are *fully disengaged*. That means a mind-blowing 71 percent of employees fall into what Towers Perrin calls a "massive middle"—a majority of workers who are constantly in flux in terms of how engaged they are with their jobs. Nonengagement has an obvious negative effect on their level of on-the-job discipline, commitment, honor, and, yes, even courage.

So what do you do about nonengagement in yourself or your team members? First, a couple of times a year you have to ask yourself and your team members if the reasons that brought you (and them) to the company or the group remain the same. Chances are they aren't. Just like in personal relationships, the thing that attracts us to a job or a department (or a person) isn't the same thing that keeps us interested. In order to build and maintain commitment and discipline, everyone—you and your team—have to explore various parts of the shared mission. That may mean job sharing and shifting and rising to new challenges.

Second, commitment is deeply personal, and that has to be evident in a work environment. "Employees care about what kind of leaders they have and leadership's focus and commitment," says Julie Gebauer, Towers Perrin Managing Director, who authored the study. People care about their ability to build skills and advance in their careers, she says, but it also matters to them what their company stands for. Commitment and discipline also relate to the reasons why you're showing up every day. If you don't know why you're getting out of bed and going off to work (aside from a paycheck, which turns out to be one of the factors least related to engagement), then you've got problems.

INVISIBLE RESULTS

Sometimes we have to make snap decisions because we need an immediate result. It's that vital you get good at making snap decisions, but you also have to know that a lot of your time will be spent plodding away at your goal. Don't let yourself get distracted because you're not seeing the fruits of your labor all at once! Sure, it's exciting to make decisions and get the immediate gratification of an instantaneous outcome. But really, do you want your heart to be racing all the time, every day? Even warriors need to step back, polish their instrument panel, and check their gear before the next battle.

It's not the quick decisions that trip people up and take them off track; it's the flawed decisions. More often than not the discouragement you feel at not seeing progress as quickly as you'd like leads to throwing in the towel and quitting. It takes a strong character to keep going in the face of what I call invisible results. Say I am trying to lose weight and I eat a cheeseburger, fries, and soda for lunch. Will I gain a pound today? No. What if I eat "clean" today—you know, veggie juice, brown rice, plenty of greens, and lean protein? Will I lose a pound? No. Not in a day. Still, there are things that are happening in my body as a result of what I am eating that I can't see (I may feel them after that double burger and fries, though). And if I eat either way—mean or clean—for a week, I will see a difference on the scale. After several weeks, I'll either fit into that new bathing suit or I won't. The outcome of the situation is up to you—you can either be confident in the invisible results that will, at some point, make themselves known, or you won't. Even confidence, an emotion, takes discipline to maintain and control.

Funny thing is, the same qualities that make you a good intuitive decision maker and a quick-thinking warrior are also the ones that help build your persistence muscle: honor, courage, and commitment. When I go into a large organization and listen to managers' concerns, they often center on the attitude newbies bring to the workforce. Newbies tend to think they want more responsibility before they can handle it, and the compensation to go with it. Trouble is, they don't even know what they don't know yet. They want the corner office, the title, the perks, the trust, and the reputation of an executive without earning these things. Grunt work, mentorships, study, practice, and experience produce invisible results.

Say I go to work every day early, 7 a.m. (about the time when the boss arrives), and work my tail off until 7 p.m., completing my tasks, asking for extra assignments, and generally being a diligent and model employee. Six months go by and I start to feel as if all this hard work isn't getting me anywhere. Why don't I have a promotion by now? Why doesn't anyone notice how hard I'm working? I don't even think the boss knows I'm around. Maybe I'll start to think, "Screw this, I'm coming it at 9 a.m. and leaving at 5 p.m. That'll show them!"

That will show them that I don't have the right stuff. Six months is no time at all. The boss sees what I'm doing. So far, so good. Now he or she wants to see if I keep it up. The truth is, there's not going to be any lavish praise coming my way for at least another six months, and only then if I deserve it. Businesses don't give out trophies just for showing up. After a year, I can go to the boss and ask him to review my performance. I have to have the results to demonstrate that I deserve a raise and a promotion. Coming in early, staying late, getting assignments done on time, taking on extra projects: All of a sudden I see the results of it, too. I know more, and I'm surer of myself. I see solutions to problems that I didn't even know existed six months ago—I'm glad I stuck with it.

Military training involves a lot of invisible results—mostly in the form of mock missions. You do the same thing over and over again so you're ready for whatever happens. For instance, one of the training missions for Afghanistan is how to help your comrades when an improvised explosive device (IED) goes off. A mock device is detonated on the side of a cliff in Nevada; it sprays a group of Marines with black talcum powder and results in several simulated casualties. Another team of Marines attempts to extract these "wounded" comrades, only to be caught in the blast of a secondary IED, eliminating most of the team. Now the Marines who are still "alive" have to figure out a way to save each other.

After you have done this or other similar practice missions for the twentieth time, you may not see much of a result. It's more like, *Okay, I just did this drill twenty times. Can I go back to base now?* But then you're in Afghanistan and an IED goes off on the side of the cliff. All of a sudden that drill experience kicks in. You know what to do and how to do it even though it's the first time you've been in this actual situation. Who says "playing pretend" is kid stuff?

BREAK POINT CASE STUDY: THE IMPORTANCE OF KEEPING PRIORITIES STRAIGHT

I first met Dana Winbush after a corporate speech I had given a few years ago. At the time, she was working in sales for a fairly large company but had a business plan of her own tucked safely away in the bottom of her desk. "I was definitely working for the man," Dana says now, of the twelve years she spent in corporate America. She's not anymore. After some coaching sessions with me, she finally moved her plan forward. In May 2010 she started her own business development firm, Intelligent Ethos, Inc., which targets entrepreneurs, start-ups, and small businesses.

Dana graduated from Vanderbilt University in 1998 with an engineering degree, "but I knew I didn't want to be an engineer," she says. Instead, she used her know-how and strategic abilities honed in engineering school to work in business development and customer relations—a field she has excelled in from the get-go. In 2006, she wrote a business plan for her own sales and marketing company but put it away. "I wasn't quite ready to make the move, but having my ideas and strategy written down gave me a certain amount of confidence in my office job," she says. That's not surprising to me—it's liberating when you know you can do something other than what you're doing, if you want to or you have to. But Dana put a few more years in "working for the man," as she put it, before implementing that plan. Part of discipline and execution is knowing in your gut when the time is right to make a move like leaving a job that looks—on paper anyway—to be secure, and hiring yourself. Not only do you need a good plan, you need to have the instinct to know when the timing is right.

"At one point I felt I was no longer moving in the direction I wanted to be going in at my last office job," says Dana. "I was still looking to make a career change and had started researching nonprofits but that was not feeling right. Then, in February 2010, a friend and colleague suggested I pull out that business plan I had written and consider whether it was my moment to strike out on my own." Dana no longer felt corporate or office jobs were as secure as they once were, given the economy and the shifting ways companies deal with downturns in business (by laying people off or reducing their hours, for example). "Working for myself, at that moment, seemed like a much safer proposition." The time was right.

Fortunately, Dana's 2006 business plan was strong—she really didn't have to make any changes to it: "It helped me understand who my customers were, and what my services would be, so I could walk away from my job confidently and know exactly who I was going to be selling to, where to find them, and how much to charge for my services. Moreover, 'churn' is very expensive, so I also had a strategy to keep customers once I had won them." What the plan didn't help her do was set up her new company's infrastructure. That detailed work was something she had to focus on before she walked away from corporate life. Again, discipline helped Dana execute *before* she called it quits on her old life.

In the few weeks before leaving her job, Dana would look at the list each day and ask herself what she was going to do toward each item on it. "Knowing what my priorities were first thing in the morning made for a very productive day. I used all the advantages I had. For instance, I lived up the street from my job so I would come home for lunch and work on items on the list. I'd spend the time with the bank or the Web guy, find the right company to supply a virtual assistant, get legal papers in order, and so on. That was my routine. After dinner and on weekends, I'd do the same thing—all the available time I had while I was still working I put toward the new business. Since it was so important to get it done, I made it a priority." In May, when Dana finally opened her doors and activated her Web site, all her ducks were in a row.

Dana's business has won clients and her smart business strategies have kept them loyal. Here are a few tips Dana's story reveals about going your own way:

1. **Had a plan:** Ideas are great, but you can't do much with them if they're not fully formed. So many of us have wonderful lightbulb moments, but you have to put them down on paper if you want the light to keep shining. Even the best ideas can dim over time—and even be forgotten—if you don't formalize them. Dana's plan was so strong it stood the test of time.

2. **Timed it right:** Timing is everything in business (and in life). Dana's business idea might have worked in 2006 but *she* wasn't ready at that point to walk away from everything, and she knew it. Yes, you should

always "strike while the iron is hot," but you have to be mentally and emotionally prepared, as well. Be mindful that a business idea and opportunity has to mesh with your own readiness to take a plunge.

3. **Devoted consistent effort:** One of the smartest things Dana did was to figure out what she needed to do to actually set up a business, and then she set about accomplishing those things before she actually started the business. Even something as seemingly trivial as making sure she had a business e-mail address was taken care of before she launched. By working on a defined list of tasks every single day, she left nothing to chance. Breaking down these jobs into daily routines made what could have been an overwhelming task very manageable.

4. **Checked in with herself:** I also like the way Dana reviewed her to-do list weekly and daily and chose to do things that propelled her forward and delegated tasks she could not handle herself (banking, legal, Web site) to the pros. But she kept tabs on them, too. Her management skills came in very handy.

5. **Knew that even the smallest positive actions create results:** Dana was very clear about the fact that each day she accomplished a task brought her closer to her goal of opening a viable business—even if opening a bank account or establishing a business address didn't seem particularly earth-shattering.

Dana Winbush demonstrated tremendous discipline and excellent execution when she left the corporate world and founded Intelligent Ethos, Inc. She took a big step that so many others would like to take (strike out on their own, transfer corporate skills to entrepreneurship). Still, even an encouraging example such as Dana's isn't enough to convince them they, too, can do it. That's why I like sharing stories of people on the front lines of wars, disasters, and other life or death situations. They offer incredible (and incredibly dramatic) lessons about discipline and execution that can be applied to more "normal" situations. Seriously, if hearing about someone running into a burning building and bringing a person out alive, or, as in the next case study, continuing to try to save a life after many people would have given up, doesn't inspire us to execute our plans once and for all, what will?

BREAK POINT CASE STUDY: CHOOSING LIFE OVER LIMB

It was devastating to watch the aftermath of the 2010 earthquake in Haiti. People who have little enough as it is saw their homes destroyed, their families separated, and loved ones lost forever. The stories I watched on the news and read in the newspaper were truly harrowing. I had seen and experienced a lot of scary and terrible things in Iraq, but this disaster seemed so much worse because it was completely unexpected and the people of Haiti weren't prepared for such a huge disaster—it would be hard for any country to have a response plan in place for something this destructive.

One story really caught my attention, because it demonstrated how important confidence, knowledge, and core values are when making life and death decisions. Now, you may never have to face such a monumental decision, but I'm sure that at some point you'll have to make a tough choice as you go from Zero to Breakthrough—breakthroughs are often the result of making the right tough decision. How will you do it?

Ask Dr. Marc Grossman, an emergency room physician at Miami's Jackson Memorial Hospital. He's also a member of the South Florida Urban Search and Rescue Task Force. The task force went to Haiti and responded to the disaster quickly. Within hours Dr. Grossman and his team were tunneling through debris at a collapsed school and miraculously found a fifteen-year-old girl who was still alive. She was pinned down by debris and her left arm was crushed under the massive weight of a piece of concrete.

Amazingly, the task force had the right gear to lift 25,000 pounds of rubble, and they could have used it to shift enough concrete and steel to free her arm. Unfortunately, there was no time to set the gear up, let alone use it to shift the debris.

"She was dying right in front of me," Grossman said. Instead, the father of two made another decision: He called a colleague at his hospital to get a quick lesson in amputation. It was the only choice he had if he were to save the life of the child who lay in front of him. The doctor gave him instructions on how to perform an amputation—directions that assumed Grossman would be working in a sterile operating room. Grossman had to take the chance anyway, knowing that he'd be doing the procedure in a cramped space filled with dirt, rocks, broken glass, and rusty metal.

In an opening less than twelve inches high, the doctor

packed a clean scalpel and slowly inched his way to the teenager. When he reached her he gave her a fast-acting sedative, and then tried to make the cut. There simply was not enough room for him to get the kind of movement he needed to cut through the bone. So Grossman backed himself out of the crevice, grabbed a surgical bone saw from his kit, and went back in. But there wasn't enough space to move the saw back and forth, either. Time was running out. Undeterred, Grossman went back out again and looked at what else the search team had brought with them. He spotted a circular saw—the kind you buy at Home Depot. Normally it was used to cut away downed tree branches, but on this day it would become Grossman's last best hope for the teen.

He grabbed the saw and quickly made his way back to the girl. He tied a tourniquet around her upper left arm and in one cut he took off her arm. As he began to pull the girl to freedom he saw that there was another girl—also alive—behind the one he had just saved. Grossman was able to pull her to safety as well. Had he not taken that risk with the circular saw, both of the girls would have died.

Okay, are you still breathing? Here are a few ways to use this incredible story when you have to make tough choices:

1. **Had fearlessness and knowledge:** Grossman wasn't afraid to find out what he needed to do to save a life. He had never done an amputation, but as a skilled doctor he had the confidence to ask an expert how to do the procedure and enough knowledge to carry it out.
2. **Showed stick-to-it determination:** When the first attempt didn't work, he did not walk away. He tried

something else, and when that didn't work, he tried again. He kept trying until he found what worked.

3. **Used creativity and open-mindedness:** Grossman was willing to think outside the box and use a tool not normally found in hospital operating rooms. When he spotted the circular saw his experience and intuition told him that it would solve the space problem he had with the other instruments—and he acted.

4. **Stood by his core principles:** Without them Grossman may have wavered, dithered, or hesitated. He did none of those things because he valued life, family, and children, and he lived by honor, courage, and commitment. Because of this, the decisions he made were not "difficult" because his values would not permit him to choose to give up.

Z2B EXERCISE: TEST YOUR PLAN

Before every mission my fellow Marines and I would rehearse our strategy so we could work out the kinks— as you'll be making many split decisions and proceeding with a certain amount of uncertainty, you don't want to have to work out the plan on the battlefield, in the office, or on the ball field. The Marines call this repetitive skills training, which I've described with many examples already (remember my flight school experience?). You can do this, too. Look, if effective decision making and successful execution of plans depend on experience, you're going to have to get some. Doing dry runs is one way to get experience. Practice might not always make perfect, but it can increase your comfort level when you're ready to suit up and go.

1. *Test your plan.* Ask a wingman or BTB to help you. Choose a day when you are well rested and have enough time to run through everything on your list thoroughly. Say you're planning on giving a presentation to a group of potential investors. Make sure you give yourself triple the amount of time you need so you can revise and run through it a second or third time. So if it's a thirty-minute presentation, schedule at least ninety minutes for the dry run.
2. *Get yourself in the groove.* Dress the part and have all your props and handouts ready. That way you can tell whether that shirt you were thinking of wearing will be uncomfortable when you're standing and walking around a room.
3. *Record yourself if possible.* Listen to the recording later and tweak it or make improvements as needed.
4. *Revise accordingly.* Ask your wingman or BTB to make note of potential problems and the best moments—*without* interrupting you. Afterward, discuss what worked and what didn't.

Z2B EXERCISE: STUDY THE MASTERS AND CREATE YOUR OWN CASE STUDIES

Part of the research phase of Zero to Breakthrough is looking to those who have gone before you, those on whose shoulders you will stand, to see how they accomplished their goals and achieved breakthrough moments. It's especially important to keep up this practice before and during the execution of your own plans. I have included a vast array of case studies in the book—from football to fashion—because I don't know what your personal goals are. I hope that more than a few of them will resonate with you.

Always seek out stories, historical descriptions, and firsthand accounts of people who have already done what you want to do. Find the best of the best—but this time, don't just read about the greatest presentation giver or public speaker, race car driver or salesperson: as you read or listen, examine the process these people used. Break it down as I have done at the end of my case studies. Ask yourself:

• Why did this person make this decision?

• What information did he have when he made it?

• What information did she lack at the time?

- Was/were the decision(s) made in a timely manner?

- What subsequent decisions did she make, and why?

- What were the results?

This kind of study strengthens your ability to recognize patterns of success and to apply them to your own situation. It's no substitute for the real thing—your own practice and experience—but conscious study can give you insight, inspiration, and answers you might not have thought of otherwise.

COURAGE IS ENDURANCE FOR ONE MOMENT MORE . . .

An unknown Marine second lieutenant in the Vietnam War spoke that famous line, and it remains relevant today. In fact, I want you to copy it down and stick it to your bathroom mirror or your computer screen—somewhere you can see it every day. Going from Zero to Breakthrough is difficult, and since you're trying for a breakthrough, every time you reach for another goal or face a tough situation there will be times when you will want to hang it all. Don't give up. Have courage and give it one more minute, then another and another. This is the perfect time to make this point because there are two things that I guarantee will happen once you start executing plans: 1) you will face obstacles, and 2) you will be scared. It's okay—I've got a few ways to get you past the roadblocks and the fears.

FLY-AWAYS

- Keep up your discipline—consistency is the key to accomplishment.

- Remember that success is achieved in two ways— the first time, and again.

- Bloom where you're planted—never sacrifice an experience because it's not your first choice.

- Agility is the ability to change direction in mid-flight when necessary.

- Trust your gut by strengthening your intuitive power.

- A quick decision is better than no decision.

- Invisible results lead to tangible accomplishments.

CHAPTER 4

When You Hit a Brick Wall,
Choose Your Weapon:
Obstacles and Challenges

> *Retreat? Hell, we're just attacking in another*
> *direction.*
>
> —ATTRIBUTED TO MAJOR GENERAL OLIVER P. SMITH,
> USMC, KOREA, DECEMBER 1950

When Major Ruvalcaba and I arrived back to base after the close call over Baghdad, we had to figure out why our missiles hadn't worked. We always did a postflight check of the Cobra, even if the aircraft hadn't been attacked. It's especially important for pilots who have flown into battle to check for damage and identify the kind of repairs needed. We also reviewed any weaknesses in our plan of attack and considered ways to make improvements for the next flight.

We found three holes in the Cobra where it had been hit by enemy fire—one under the cockpit, one in the tail boom (the back end of the aircraft), and another in a rotor blade. The round that hit the cockpit had disabled the weapons system. We were oblivious to the damage while we were flying, even though we knew we'd been shot at. Unless you get an indication in the cockpit like Szepesy did, you don't know when you're hit. At any rate, the Cobra could be fixed; the real blessing was that the round didn't hit one of us, as it easily might have.

Aside from checking the damage, we went over the flight with each other and talked about how we would react next time if the same thing happened. What could we have done better? What would we have done if we had been shot down—there's protocol for that, of course, but sometimes protocol isn't always possible to follow during a warfare situation. Just talking about it, reviewing what happened, and coming to an agreement on the pluses and minuses of our reactions was helpful and comforting, too. Reviewing helps you move forward.

POSTFLIGHT CHECKS HELP PREVENT FUTURE OBSTACLES

Postmortems are crucial to making progress and revising future plans for the best outcomes. They're critical in business and life. I always analyze situations I find myself in; moreover, I look for ways to make them turn out better the next time. It's kind of like seeing the obstacles in real time so you can deal with them when they're thrown up in front of you in the future. You can think on your feet if you don't let trouble knock you down.

Sometimes I take a little flack in my personal life when I want to go back over unpleasant situations, but it pays off. When I have had miscommunications with a colleague or friend, for example, I like to review the conversation first with myself and then with the other person to find out how the misunderstanding occurred. I find it funny how few people seem to like to do this; in fact, most of them loathe it. In my view, you can't "move on" until you've cleared the air, identified what went wrong, and addressed it. The next time a similar situation comes up our communication and listening skills are sharper.

The same goes for my business dealings. After I give a speech, I always watch it if I have a video of it, or at least listen to it. I pay attention not only to my delivery, to identify what worked and what I could have done better, but I also pay very close attention to how the audience reacted and to what and why. When did they laugh? (Keep those moments in—laughter is good for connecting with an audience.) When did they moan or react in any other way? What didn't they react to? Those "dead zones" are important to find and eliminate. These postmortems allow me to constantly improve my presentations. I also like asking people to fill out response cards after a workshop—the opinions of clients are crucial to honing my skills and keeping material relevant and fresh.

Same goes for my marketing material. I generate a lot of postcards and other mailing material, e-mail newsletters, Internet postings, videos, and so on. The only way I can get a read on what's working (what's best addressing my clients' needs and what's connecting me to more business) is to figure out a way to measure the results, collect data on who's responding to what, and make judgments and decisions based on the past performance of these materials. Why did this postcard win more responses than another? Because it had a picture of me in my flight suit (positive response) rather than a business suit or my military uniform (not as big of a response). Then I adjust my strategy for the next mailing accordingly.

Keeping a critical eye on all personal and professional dealings has helped me be more effective and has also taught me not take every piece of criticism or disappointment personally. I'll talk more about that in this chapter, because one thing is certain: Taking things personally can make us our own worst enemy. If I took every nonreaction to a speech, slight, or snub personally, I'd become reactionary in my thinking. You know: "Everyone is out to get me." "Don't they appreciate the effort I go to?" I would be blind to the gifts and blessings I was provided with.

I was asked to speak to a group of corporate managers at a large international bank. One of the issues that came up was learning from successes and mistakes. Let me tell you, these guys (and gals) were a little like politicians. The many layers of corporate bureaucracy had them doing postmortems all right— big time. A team would study a project and issue a report, then the team leader would form a committee of people outside the group to study the study, and then another committee would be formed to report on the study (are you still with me?). Several weeks (sometimes months) would pass, and finally a few ideas might filter down to the people who were responsible for the original project. Sometimes not. Often these postmortem reports would get stuck in a committee. By that time the team had already moved on to another assignment and usually it was too late to use any of the insights gleaned from the postmortem committee's suggestions.

Nimble businesses get down to the business of postmortem right away, as soon as they see results. They look for patterns of success or failure and apply what they learned to the next challenge immediately. Small businesses, good ones, do this all the time because they have neither the manpower nor the luxury of time to form study groups. This is one of the many ways that being lean and mean gives a small company an advantage over a big one. They have to look at a result or a situation, analyze it, and make a decision quickly, in real time.

The bank had to streamline the process, get rid of the committees, and put the postmortem responsibility back with the original team. They needed to cut out all the middlemen and respond to project results much like a small business would—immediately upon receiving the results. Was the marketing outreach effective? Did it bring in new business, and if so, how much and was it worth the costs associated with the plan? I told them that if this strategy didn't improve the process of evaluating their marketing plans, they could go back to the old way. It did work, and the bank never looked back at their old bulky way of doing postmortems.

You're probably wondering how I went from Baghdad and holes in a Cobra to analyzing conversations, to consulting with a big bank performing a postmortem. These are examples of the sort of challenges that people face all the time (sometimes literally, sometimes figuratively, of course—everyone isn't getting their helicopter shot down). They slow you down, sure, but that doesn't mean you have to stop in your tracks. Taking a detour to look at what just happened is not retreat; it's smart.

> Every person who has grown to any degree of usefulness, every person who has grown to distinction, almost without exception has been a person who has risen by overcoming obstacles, by removing difficulties, by resolving that when he met discouragement he would not give up.
>
> —BOOKER T. WASHINGTON

STRONG BODY EQUALS STRONG MIND: THE CRUCIBLE FOR CIVILIANS

When Marine recruits enter boot camp, they go through a rigorous period of physical training, or PT, that helps them meet the stringent strength and endurance standards of the Corps. A drill instructor leads platoons through a series of demanding exercises including push-ups; medicine ball drills; bungee jumping or repelling; sled drags; and "suicide runs," also known as confidence runs. At some point during camp they'll also be put through obstacle courses, circuit courses, and three-, five-, or ten-mile conditioning marches. This training readies them for the battlefield.

Combat Confidence: Failure is *not* your final destination.

There's one more thing a person has to complete before becoming a Marine. He or she has to go through a "culminating event" called the Crucible, a harrowing physical and emotional ordeal. For fifty-four straight hours, recruits are pushed to their limits as they face every conceivable obstacle. It's only when a recruit completes the Crucible successfully that he or she earns the right to be called a Marine.

The Crucible is tough. You have to go, go, go, with little sleep. The point of the exercise is deprivation and physical challenge, and its purpose is to simulate combat. Going in, I wasn't the best runner in the world, but during Officer Candidate School my running power and speed had increased so much I was able to navigate every obstacle and excel. In fact, I became one of the fastest in my platoon because of the upper body strength I'd developed. When we crossed the finish line, I thought, "Wow, we have come such a long way." At the very end of the Crucible, when you pass the finish line, the platoon staff lines you up for the Eagle, Globe, and Anchor ceremony. You're dirty and smelly and hungry and exhausted, and that's when they say, "You've earned the right to be called a Marine." I still get choked up thinking about it.

If there is one thing the Crucible taught me it is that physical strength and stamina are important for success whether you're a Marine or a civilian. The body and mind are intertwined, and if you're tired or lack fortitude, intellectual challenges, especially those in business, will be that much harder to meet and overcome.

Say you're working toward an advanced degree or going back to school after a long hiatus; planning a new business or expanding an existing one; or setting up a Web site or researching new technology for an upcoming project. Why would you need to be physically fit for any of these sedentary jobs? Numerous studies have shown that regular exercise improves your cognitive abilities, including memory, decision making, motivation, attention and concentration, and the speed in which you can solve problems (quick thinking).

These happen to be all the skills you need to work your way around potential obstacles, including negative self-talk, external critics, competitors, losses, refusals, failed attempts, unexpected predicaments, and false starts. Not to mention all the potential roadblocks the physical world presents, from snowstorms to tornadoes and stalled subway cars to traffic jams.

The ancient Greek philosopher Plato wrote, "In order for man to succeed in life, God provided him with two means, education and physical activity. Not separately, one for the soul and the other for the body, but for the two together. With these two means, man can attain perfection." I'm not sure about perfection, but you'll have a better chance of getting over hurdles if you train both your mind and body to be strong. Are you willing to push yourself beyond the limits of your perceived capabilities?

According to John J. Ratey, MD, author of *Spark: The Revolutionary New Science of Exercise and the Brain*, exercising is the single most powerful thing we can do to boost, build, and maintain our brainpower. Ratey describes a study that found aerobic exercise increases brain cell capacity in certain areas by as much as 30 percent immediately following the workout. When I give a talk to a large group—especially one that I haven't met before—I do a much better job if I've worked out beforehand. Not only does it reduce stress, it makes me feel sharper and more enthusiastic. That excitement transfers to the audience and everyone has a good time.

I'm not suggesting you set up an obstacle course in your backyard and sleep in a tent for fifty-four hours with only crackers and water for sustenance. But I do recommend that you discover or rediscover your passion for exercise. Devoting thirty minutes to an hour to vigorous exercise at the beginning of your day—running, walking briskly, bicycle riding, stair climbing, dancing, or classic calisthenics—does make you sharper and better able to handle the day no matter what or who pops up from behind a boulder.

HOW THE WALL WAS BUILT DETERMINES HOW YOU TAKE IT DOWN

There are three kinds of obstacles: those that you create yourself; those that are constructed by the competition or "enemy;" and those that are due to natural causes (environmental or natural conditions, events outside of your control, actual physical obstructions). Learn to distinguish between them and you're halfway to beating them back.

At this point in Zero to Breakthrough, you've started to eliminate or at least drastically reduce three of the ways you self-impose obstacles on your progress. By concentrating on your passions, identifying your talents, and researching and preparing for a goal, you've focused on your mission. This is a breakthrough in and of itself, and many people don't even get that far. So give yourself a pat on the back.

People who lack clarity can't wade through the bombardment of choices they're faced with. They get confused and overwhelmed, are pulled in different directions, and ultimately wind up stuck right where they are. Lack of clarity tends to make people distracted and able to respond only to the most urgent obligations. What's worse is lack of knowledge and planning—the guy who hasn't done his homework is completely unprepared to even *approach* something new. It all seems out of reach and unattainable.

When you are focused on your mission and have laid the groundwork through work, practice, and research, any roadblocks or problems can be addressed with logic and knowledge. I have a friend who's in the process of building a house on a tricky lot—there is a steep hill on one side and a natural stream on the other that her local township considers a protected wetland. This makes positioning the house problematic. The setbacks (the amount of space between the house and the waterway and cliff edge) have to be just right to be safe, practical, and in keeping with state and local environmental rules. She had to go before what seemed like an endless number of community board meetings, go back—literally—to the drawing board and redo plans, resubmit them, and continuously revise building schedules.

She met every obstacle with enthusiasm—figuring out how to get this darn house up was more than half the fun of getting it built. By the time she got the permits and the framing started, I sensed she was a tiny bit depressed. That is, until she had to help the contractor figure out how to cantilever a deck over the stream. Turned out the obstacles were what made the project enjoyable to my friend. "Outsmarting" the house became a game that provided both pleasure and excitement. Sure, like my friend, you have to give time and sweat to solving problems. However, the confidence and clarity you have makes finding answers that much less complicated. In fact, finding a way around the obstacle becomes part of the satisfaction of your work.

But (you knew that was coming, right?) just because you're intellectually and physically prepared for the challenges that lie ahead doesn't mean you're not creating obstacles that keep you from flying high.

Excuse Me, But Could You Get Out of Your Way?

I had a 6:45 a.m. flight and I planned to get there at 6 a.m., but I was late getting up and procrastinated a bit and ended up making it to the airport at 6:15 a.m. Bad planning on my part—and when I saw at least a hundred people standing in line at the skycap, and then checked out the even longer line inside the terminal, I knew I was in trouble. Getting through the line and making my flight in half an hour, just post-9/11, was not going to be easy. I could pitch a fit and get thrown out of the airport; that wouldn't be productive. I could go home and fly tomorrow, but I'd miss an important engagement. Both of these options would be shooting myself in the foot.

Instead, I walked up to an airline ticket agent who was standing by herself, showed her my ticket, flashed a smile, and asked her if she could do anything to help me out. She looked at her watch and said, "You're going to miss your flight—you'll have to rebook it." All I wanted to know was whether I'd make my engagement. Yes, I'd make it, if I was willing to stand on two lines, take what they gave me (two stopovers), and be willing to make the trip an all-nighter—as soon as I stepped off the final flight I'd have to go right to my engagement. Did this sound appealing to me? No, it sounded exhausting.

But okay, I did it. It was a pretty nasty series of flights, and I wasn't able to get a lot of sleep or prep time in. There was a lot of running from one gate to another in airports. But I was willing to do whatever I had to do (including endure all sorts of discomfort) to make my presentation—and since it was a problem of my own making, I had to live up to it even if I didn't like admitting that. Many of us refuse to take the necessary steps to get ourselves out of a jam—and if that's you, you have to change your thinking.

Obviously, the postmortem on this one didn't take long. I said to myself, Vernice, you've got to set your alarm for the proper time and get up when it goes off. No excuses. I have to own up to one of my fatal flaws—really loving to stay in that bed—and deal with it. What are your fatal flaws—the ones you trip over time and again? Get with them and get rid of them (or make do and do what you need to do if you can't).

Hello? I'm About to Trip Over That Chip on Your Shoulder

Combat Confidence: If you think, project, and behave as if people don't like you because you're *[fill in the blank]* over time, guess what? They'll grant your wish.

We've been forming a set of beliefs from the time we were born. These beliefs change over time: With experience come new beliefs; old ones fade away while others continue to strengthen. That's life—the fact that we form ideas and develop concepts and opinions distinguishes us from the other creatures in the animal kingdom. Problem is, some of the most tightly held attitudes and convictions may not be based in reality—and they could be limiting us. Our thoughts can be some of our biggest obstacles. If we can identify our beliefs, be honest about them, and separate them from reality, we can make better choices and become much less "hung up" on the ideas that hold us back.

For instance, people say to me, "Wow, Vernice, you're black; you're a woman; you were in the Marine Corps. Have you ever faced any discrimination?" Dramatic pause. Probably. Maybe. Maybe not. If there was friction, it could have been because I was happy in the morning, or could bench press more than they could, or because I was black or a woman. Honestly, I didn't care. My job was to be the best pilot I could be. Lives depended on it. Who's depending on you and who are you giving power to?

I've rarely let any "ism" get in my way. Besides, I have built up my armor (how could I not—it's my last name), so it's a rare person who can put chinks in it. When you allow others to become false obstacles because of what they *might think or do think*, you're in trouble. For example, as a copilot I had to sell my flight plan and get my crew on my side. My job was to protect people and come back alive. You have to have confidence and use logic. I can't think about whether the other pilot doesn't like me because of my femaleness or my blackness. When you confront negativity, at first you may feel like a bag of rags. If you get criticism, it might be legitimate—go back and do your own postmortem. Take the truth, use it, and let the rest fall away. Moreover, don't fall back on tired stereotypes or second guessing someone else's motivations. That's way too easy, and it's never productive—and usually wrong. Look yourself in the eye and be honest about your strengths and limitations.

Most important, never assume you know what other people are thinking. Don't let your assumptions about what another person is doing, saying, or thinking control your own reactions, decisions, or behavior.

I live near my old base, and there's a movie theater that's within walking distance. So I'm always running into old buddies—it's a nice way to catch up and stay connected. Recently my mom and I walked over to the theater to see a movie. I spotted a guy I knew in the lobby, someone whom I had joked around with on the base. We had been pretty good buddies. Naturally, I waved. He looked away. Weird. Then he turned again, caught my eye, and I waved again. This time he waved quickly and promptly turned his back on me. He seemed to be going out of his way to avoid me. It was a cold reality check—but not the kind I had initially pictured.

At that moment, I took it personally (was all that joking around on the base an act?). I caught myself before I confronted him and made an awkward situation even more embarrassing. Instead, I flipped the script: As I thought about the encounter more carefully (and less emotionally), I realized that first of all, his behavior was his stuff, not mine. And then it occurred to me that he could have been cheating on his wife.

> **Combat Confidence:** Prepare for the competition because, baby, the competition is preparing for you!

In fact, he was acting like a guilty and embarrassed man. I didn't know the person he was with, and I had never met his wife. I was making all these self-centered assumptions when the reality more likely had nothing to do with me (except maybe that he was upset that one of his old buds would find him out). Most important, though, is that his behavior *has no impact on my life.* Even if the most unpleasant things I thought about his actions were true, how could they possibly hurt my goals or me?

The Other Guy Obstacle

> **Combat Confidence:** If you remember nothing else about Zero to Breakthrough, remember this: *Acknowledge obstacles, but don't give them power.*

One thing you're taught as a Marine is to never underestimate your enemy. If you do, it could mean your life. That's quite an obstacle. The other guy—your competitor, for example—may well be a real obstacle. That's why underestimating him is a bad idea. Thinking that the opposition is no competition is giving them an opening and weakens your own resolve. It's when you're not paying attention that obstacles become accidents.

There's a war legend that all Marines know—it happened during the Battle of Belleau Wood during World War I in June of 1918, near the Marne River in France. The Germans were holed up in the woods waiting to invade. The Marines had to attack six times before successfully ousting them. Despite the fact that the Americans were undersupplied, they managed to fight off parts of five different divisions of Germans, often using only their bayonets and hand-to-hand combat.

The story goes that when all else failed, the Marines bit the Germans—that's right, with their teeth—earning them the name *Teufelhunde*, or "dogs of the devil." Marines are still called Devil Dogs to this day. An official German report classified the Marines as "vigorous, self-confident, and remarkable marksmen." Sounds about right. I guess the Germans underestimated the Marines. Since it's not a good idea to bite the person in the next cubicle or bring a bayonet to your next sales call, you have to use a few other strategies to stay on your game.

- *Acknowledge but don't acquiesce.* Take note of who's trying to hold you back, but don't give them power or let them steal your joy. My mom used to say to me, "Baby, pay him (or her) no mind," when someone was mean to me as a schoolgirl. I used to think that meant to ignore the nasty people, but it really doesn't. As I got a little older I realized that this bit of wisdom meant that you should recognize the person's behavior for what it is, but without letting it affect your mood or upset your plans. It's out there, you know it, and you go about your business. My momma's one smart lady, don't you think?

- *Develop your peripheral vision without losing the main target.* Focus is powerful, but tunnel vision can make you weak. So many successful people I know, from managers to small businesspeople, military officers to professional athletes, believe the key to accomplishment is found in their ability to concentrate on a single purpose. Hey, I've said it since the beginning: A long-term vision gives you and your group a shared sense of direction and common goals. A grand vision energizes people and keeps them "signed on" for the long haul.

  A popular example of this phenomenon is when President John F. Kennedy committed to send a man to the moon by the end of the 1960s. This historic and future-thinking vision galvanized everyone, from retired office workers to young schoolchildren. This common purpose and excitement united technology, banking, and science to realize the vision and ultimately allowed the United States to win the "space race" before the Soviet Union.

There *are* risks involved in thinking this way. If you're not careful, focus can turn into tunnel vision. When you fixate on a single vision and see it as the only acceptable goal, you can really miss what's going on around you, on the periphery—both threats *and* emerging opportunities. Think about driving down the highway. Before you change lanes you check the rearview mirror to make sure it's safe. If you didn't—kaboom! While you're on the road, you glance over to the left and right, don't you? If you didn't, you wouldn't see the signs and exits for gas, food, or lodging.

There also may be a tendency to bet the whole farm on the vision, or to have a false sense of security. It was the "I've got a great plan and I can see the finish line" thinking that enabled the turtle to win the race while the rabbit slept. So look around once in a while—check out what the competition's doing, see what's on the sidelines along with what's on the horizon.

It's not "slow and steady wins the race" that's important about this story, because in today's high-speed environment being methodical isn't always a possible or positive winning strategy. It's that the rabbit thought his plan and execution, his abilities, so far outstripped the tortoise's that he simply didn't think that it would be necessary to keep an eye on what was happening outside of himself. For example, I'm pretty confident in my abilities as a speaker. Still, I always look to see what other people in my business are doing. I don't obsess over it, but I try to learn from it. I keep an eye on all my competitors because people can constantly improve. They innovate and come up with ideas when you least expect it. I don't want to be caught up short.

- *Deal with critics and naysayers with kind persistence (okay, stubbornness with a smile).* As the only girl in the family, having three brothers was an experience and a journey all its own. I wanted to be as strong and independent as they were, and at the same time I wanted to be my own girl. For instance, when I was about thirteen I wanted to play the trumpet in my seventh-grade music class. I was simply in love with brass instruments. My mom didn't think it was a great idea. "Oh, baby, you'll get a red ring around your lips. How about the flute?" Mom played the flute, and my best friend, Tracie, was playing the flute. So what did that mean? Thank you. That's right, the flute.

No way was I going to play a flute. I had discovered a old clunky trombone out in the garage; it didn't even have a mouthpiece. Still, I'd go out there and put my little lips on the place where the mouthpiece was supposed to go and blow and slide and blow and slide. My dad would come out and say, "Vernice, leave that trombone alone." You know I was playing with it every chance I could get, right?

When I got to ninth grade, I asked the band director, Mr. Ryan, if I could be in the trombone section. He said, "Vernice, you don't play trombone, you play flute." These people and their flute obsession! "I know, I know, Mr. Ryan," I said, "but we have one in the garage and I've been practicing with it."

"Okay, calm down, Vernice," he said. "Why don't you keep practicing and take some lessons, and come concert band season, I'll audition you. If you're good enough, you can play in the band."

"Deal!" I said. I ran home and was disappointed that my mom and dad were still out. I think I watched the door so hard its hinges would have melted if my parents hadn't walked in the door—finally—at 7:30. What *took* them so long? "Mom, Dad, Mr. Ryan said I have to play trombone," I fibbed (artists have poetic license, don't they?). "Vernice, what are you talking about?" my father said. I had no time for conversation! "Mom, we don't have much time, there's a trombone in the garage, and I need to get a mouthpiece for it. Can you take me to the music store tonight?"

"Vernice, it's 7:30; the store closes at 8:00."

"I know, it only takes twenty minutes to get there, we can make it," I pleaded.

They threw me in the car and we drove up to the local music store; we picked out two mouthpieces and a couple of music books. When we got home I immediately went upstairs and began to teach myself to play trombone for real. Come audition day, Mr. Ryan was blown away. "Wow, great job, Vernice. Who did you take lessons from?"

"I didn't take any lessons. I taught myself." Six months later, I made all West Tennessee. The next year I made all state, all state jazz, and all state orchestra, and I was a member of the Memphis Youth Symphony Orchestra.

The next time someone says no, just keep saying yes through your actions, commitment, and attitude.

BREAK POINT CASE STUDY: LOSE IT AND LOVE IT

I had dinner with a couple of colleagues and Doris Buffett, the great financier Warren Buffett's sister. Several months before, I had met her at a conference. Confession: At the start of the conference I didn't know exactly who Doris was but I wanted to help her with her project to mentor kids. All I knew was that this regal-looking, very pretty older woman was telling some great stories, and we were all having a great time. At dinner, the conversation turned to the economy, which at the time was acting pretty unpredictably if the stock market was any indication.

Doris related the story of what happened to her on Black Monday, when the stock market crashed. On October 19, 1987, markets around the world crashed in quick succession, beginning in Hong Kong and spreading west to Europe and, finally, the United States. By the time the Dow Jones had fallen 508 points, the rest of the world markets had already been severely devalued. "When I woke up that morning, I had $12 million securely tucked in the bank," I remember her saying. At the end of the day, when the stock market closed, she was in debt to the tune of $2 million.

"My family had two rules about money," she told us. "Number one is do not lose money, and number two is do not lose money." She broke both rules in one day. Her family, including her brother Warren, didn't bail her out. She didn't expect them to. In fact, Doris learned that her mother, Leila, wrote in her daybook after the crash, "Don't give Doris a cent."

Instead of whining about the unfairness of it all, Doris rented out rooms in her home, sold her personal jewelry and antiques, began paying her debt, cut back, and made sacrifices just as any other responsible person would do when their finances come under attack. And Doris Buffett made it through, like she always had. You see, there's a backstory here. Doris had endured years of the worst psychological abuse from her mother (which Warren and her younger sister bore witness to), four failed marriages, a falling-out with her children, and severe depression.

The crash happened when Doris was sixty years old—a time of life when many people think about retirement and kicking back. So it wasn't exactly easy to start over, but she did. "There was a fellow I knew who was in the same position as I," she said. "The only difference between us was that I was no longer working, and he had a job making more than $100,000 a year. I couldn't imagine making that much money back then," Doris said. "Yet that man committed suicide over his losses."

Doris was living modestly until 1996, when, at age seventy, she inherited millions of dollars of Berkshire Hathaway that went to her when her mother died. The newfound fortune gave Doris a chance to live comfortably, but its primary function is to make the lives of others better. The Sunshine Lady Foundation was established soon after her inheritance, and over the past fourteen years, she has used it to donate more than $100 million to charities serving battered women and children, underprivileged and sick children, and other causes dear to her heart. She told us her goal was to give everything away before she dies. "I'm grateful for this joy at the end of my life," she said.

I'm not going to pretend that Doris didn't have advantages that few enjoy—how many of you expect to inherit millions of dollars in stock? But remember, Doris didn't count on that inheritance; she took the hand that life dealt her and rolled with it. Her attitude, despite financial losses and hardship, was one of gratitude: To whom much is given, much is expected. The methods she used to overcome obstacles can be used by anyone, no matter what their family history or financial situation is.

1. **Did what needed to be done:** After losing her savings and investments in the stock market crash, Doris Buffett took everything she had of value and sold it. She faced an obstacle that was unmovable (losing all her money), at least temporarily, and set about in another direction (selling what she had of value).

2. **Didn't make circumstances worse:** Doris modified her plans and created a life that was just as rich and happy, if not quite as lavish, as she had before. Some people call this "making lemonade." That works for me. Bottom line, she did not let the obstacle get in the way of creating a worthwhile life for herself.

3. **Made obstacles into opportunities:** Instead of feeling bitter about her childhood and the heartache it likely led to (failed marriages, strained relationships with her children, depression) Doris "flipped the script" of her life. When she received her inheritance, at age seventy, she started a foundation to help others overcome the obstacles in *their* lives.

Obstacles can be amazing learning and innovation tools, too. Overcoming can translate into coming up with brilliant ideas. Always ask yourself:

- By getting over this obstacle, will I be able to solve other problems?

- Is this really an obstacle, or am I just seeing it as one?

- What can I learn from this so-called obstacle?

BREAK POINT CASE STUDY:
BIG C IS FOR BIG COURAGE

At just thirty-one years old, actress and photographer Kris Carr was diagnosed with epithelioid hemangioendothelioma (EHE), a rare, mysterious, and incurable form of cancer. As the universe would have it, it was discovered in stage four, which means that cancer cells have metastasized, or spread to other organs or throughout the body. EHE is a slow-moving vascular cancer in the lining of the blood vessels, liver, and lungs, and it is so rare that only 0.01 percent of the cancer population has it. Only about two hundred to three hundred cases are diagnosed in America every year, and the cause is unknown. Since it's so uncommon, there aren't any drug companies or researchers looking into it.

Kris was living in New York City, working on her acting career, photographing other actors, and generally having a great time as a single girl in the city. In the middle of all this, the music just stopped. She had the Big C. Obstacle. There were tears for sure, lots of sobbing and sleeping and depression-enhanced lethargy, and of course panicking—"I'm gonna die." But in a fairly short period of time, Kris picked herself up off the floor (where she found herself quite often in the beginning, in tears), located a bunch of really good doctors she liked and trusted, and took steps to keep herself healthy.

"The catalyst for me was that there was no cure, no treatment, really there were zero Western alternatives," she says.

"If someone had said, 'oh, here's the cure,' I would have done it—chemo, surgery, whatever—and gone back to where I was. Because there were no options, I had to create options for myself."

Another pretty cool thing happened. In her drive to find the right way to live with stage four cancer, Kris realized that there was not one place where young women like her who had cancer or other health issues could go to vent, exchange information, and connect. This prompted her to make a documentary about her cancer journey, called *Crazy Sexy Cancer*, and to write a book for women in her same situation, called *Crazy Sexy Cancer Tips*. Two more books followed, *Crazy Sexy Cancer Survivor* and *Crazy Sexy Diet*.

The film and book turned out to be game changers. First, there were no other books or films quite like what Kris had created—funny and irreverent but authentic and also reassuring and informative (if you know a woman with cancer, get them a copy of both). "The world opened for me—I was on *Oprah*, the national news, and lots of other television outlets. I got another book deal, speaking engagements, workshops—so many things happened I could barely keep up with the success," she says.

Based on the response she got, Kris knew she was on to something. Women craved the information and point of view she provided. Two Web sites followed, crazysexycancer. com and crazysexylife.com. The brand and business has taken off—she's a regular on the speaking circuit, offers wellness boot camps and seminars, and continues to provide support and information through her Web outlets. Today, Kris, with her Crazy Sexy brand, is a trusted source for those living with cancer, but it's also about veganism, raw food, nutrition, and overall wellness and spirituality. The Crazy Sexy brand is growing bigger every day—and none of it would have happened had it not been for a big, scary obstacle that Kris was able to see as an opportunity.

"When you're told you have stage four cancer, you think, 'Oh, that's a death sentence.' That was unacceptable. For me the question became, How can I get around it or push it off? It's not that it was easy to make peace with my cancer—it wasn't, and it took time. On the other hand, I had to count my blessings. What was *not* an obstacle about my cancer? It's slow moving, for one thing. It's not taking me out today and it's not taking me out tomorrow. It's also part of me, and how is it productive to hate a part of yourself?" she says.

That positive but pragmatic attitude is part of Kris's business model. She also shows her clients, readers, and followers how to embrace the same attitude—whatever you think is wrong about you either exists or it doesn't. If it's real, it's part of you, so you have to make it work. "The happier I got about the condition I was in, the more successful I got and the more successful my readers and clients became."

From a devastating diagnosis, Kris essentially created an entirely new life and a vibrant and growing business. In the process, she found her true calling. If it weren't for cancer, none of this would have happened. How did she do it?

1. **Felt the pain:** When a nasty obstacle gets in your way, what's wrong with being aware of the sadness and anxiety in your heart (and crying if you want to)? If you deny yourself the opportunity to recognize when something hurts on an emotional level, you're just

burying it. It could show up later, at an inconvenient time, and with a vengeance.

2. **Saw what could be done about it:** Kris wasted no time in finding the best experts to fill her in on what was going on inside her body. She also didn't depend on those experts; she took matters into her own hands. Through research and talking to alternative practitioners and other cancer survivors, she formulated a way to live and eat that has helped her stay healthy and energetic.

3. **Stayed realistic:** Kris didn't give into magical thinking ("why me?") or use cancer as an excuse to live at less than her full potential. She's also very careful about not falling into cancer platitudes, which keeps her grounded. "I'm very careful about not calling cancer a gift, which is something I would give to my family and friends. However, I do see cancer as a blessing, and that's a different thing entirely."

4. **Stayed tuned in to the environment:** It's not uncommon for a challenging obstacle to make us go inward and become too self-absorbed or reticent to stay a part of the world. Kris refused to do that—and because of her sense of belonging in the world she saw a need in cancer and wellness worlds that was not being addressed: a place for women with cancer to exchange information, stay connected, communicate, and get better.

5. **Turned the obstacle into passion and purpose:** Wow. Imagine finding a giant, unmovable boulder in the middle of the road. Instead of spending useless hours trying

to push it out of the way or going back home, you instead turn it into the most fantastic in-demand boulder ever, right where it is. That's what Kris did. She seized the moment. And in doing so she proved that a great business idea, a purpose, and a great legacy can come from anywhere, if we just have the courage to see it.

So go ahead and let an obstacle throw you for a loop. Just get up as soon as you can, and see what you can make of it. If you want to get really good at facing down obstacles, you have to be honest about your strengths and weaknesses and you have to learn how to not let stuff get to you. Here are two exercises to help you do just that.

Z2B EXERCISE: GET HONEST

Okay, grab a pen and your journal or a pad of paper. Sit down and get comfortable—you need some quiet time for this exercise. You don't have to share what you write down with anyone (which is why you shouldn't do it on a computer). This is for your eyes only.

Think about the beliefs and behaviors you have that are obstacles. Own up to them, and then get over yourself. For instance, the fact that I'm a chick in the military could have been an easy excuse whenever I failed or decided to take someone else's behavior as an excruciating personal slight—but how insulting to myself and to other women would that be? And it would accomplish what, exactly? You see, saying you can't overcome a perceived "ism" is reducing yourself to a mythological stereotype.

Likewise, negative beliefs about money can keep you from earning more of it ("money is evil," "rich people are greedy and mean," and so on). What are yours? Bad work habits can keep you from being recognized for your talents (showing up late, missing deadlines, and so on). Do you have any?

Once you've figured out your personal obstacles, can you think of at least two ways of breaking down each obstacle? For example, if you're chronically late, are there any strategies, like setting your clocks and watch thirty minutes ahead or asking a friend or hiring a message service to give you reminder calls at certain times so you're not walking into meetings fifteen minutes after they've begun?

Z2B EXERCISE: FLIP THE SCRIPT

We all talk ourselves into believing all sorts of false beliefs. I did at it the movie theater when a Marine buddy snubbed me. At first I took it personally because I thought that his behavior had something to do with me. Here's the truth: Negative assumptions can infect your attitude to the point where you might start accusing people (at least in your mind) of imagined transgressions before they've even said hello. There's no profit in that. How about next time you catch yourself thinking that way, stop, acknowledge the person or event, and turn your thoughts around? "He doesn't like me" becomes "He seems preoccupied, and it's not my problem." "She did that on purpose to hurt me" becomes "Too bad she seems so angry today; I'm going to do what I have to do on my own and hope she feels better tomorrow."

Remember these three things:
1. Never assume you know what the other guy is thinking.
2. What you assume the other guy is thinking probably is inaccurate.
3. What difference does it make anyway what anyone is thinking—dwelling on things you can't possibly know is a form of negative self-talk, a genuine obstacle for achieving breakthrough moments.

"THE BENDED KNEE IS NOT A TRADITION OF OUR CORPS"

General Alexander A. Vandegrift, USMC, spoke that line near the end of a speech to the Senate Naval Affairs Committee on May 5, 1946, which has come to be known, appropriately, as the "bended knee speech." During his tenure as commandant of the Corps, the Marines were nearly disbanded, as post–World

War II discussions on restructuring the Army, Navy, and Marines opened the possibility of diminishing both the role and the mission of the Corps. Vandegrift wasn't going to let that happen.

His speech won the support of Congress, and the Marine Corps has stayed autonomous and intact—and vitally important to this nation's security—to this day. As the Navy and both President Harry Truman and General Dwight Eisenhower supported the change, it was quite an obstacle to overcome. Didn't matter—General Vandegrift was not going to surrender without a fight. He would not go down on bended knee.

Like all Marines, Vandegrift knew that every obstacle prompts a choice. You can find a way to overcome it, or you can give up without trying. I understand that knocking down every roadblock is easier said than done—no one is offering you a money-back guarantee. But I do know one thing: If you don't try, the roadblock stays in place. If you do try, chances are that, eventually, you'll see your way clear. I do know that approaching a problem head-on leads to discovery and, ultimately, victory on some level.

So what choice will you make? Will you have prepared for the challenges ahead, and do you have the discipline to do what's necessary to face them? Can you avoid giving even the worst circumstances power over you? Or will you refuse to make the bended knee a tradition? I hope so.

FLY-AWAYS

- See obstacles as opportunities.

- Acknowledge obstacles, but don't give them power.

- Remember that failure is not your final destination.

- Review what went wrong so you can avoid it in the future.

- Treat critics with respect and kindness—they are giving you a gift.

- Keep your mind and body in shape.

- Get rid of the chip on your shoulder.

- Prepare for the competition because the competition is preparing for you.

- Don't assume you know what other people are thinking.

- Develop peripheral vision.

CHAPTER 5

Dark Corners and Blind Spots: Fear and Focus

We're surrounded. That simplifies our problem of getting to these people and killing them.

—LIEUTENANT GENERAL LEWIS BURWELL "CHESTY" PULLER, USMC, NOVEMBER 1950, DURING THE CHOSIN RESERVOIR CAMPAIGN

One night when my partner and I were out on patrol in Nashville, we caught a "burglary in progress" call. At the time I was still a rookie; my partner was a much more experienced cop. Still, I'd been through enough car and foot chases, arrests, and domestic disputes (sometimes when I knew guns other than my own were present) to feel pretty confident about walking into a situation that could turn deadly. We put the siren on and were off to a warehouse in a desolate commercial part of town.

An alarm had gone off in the building, so we weren't responding to a 911 call initiated by a person. We could be walking into any number of situations—a group of people could be involved in a theft, a lone criminal could be at work, a homeless person might have broken in to escape the heat for the night, or it could be a false alarm. When we arrived at the entrance to the building, the doors were locked. After looking around the perimeter of the structure, we couldn't see any obvious signs of a break-in. There was always the roof, but we were going inside first. We cut the lock and proceeded with caution, guns drawn.

It was not completely dark inside but shadowy and dim. The building was filled with huge boxes of clothing stacked one on top of another. Large piles of unpacked clothes also lay in large fabric mountains, which made the space feel really creepy—and dangerous, too, as one or more individuals easily could have been hiding in any number of places: behind stacks of boxes, under a pile of clothing. We carefully and quietly worked our way around the area, using our flashlights to illuminate dark corners, securing areas as we went.

Somewhere in the darkness and dust, I heard a noise; something or someone had moved. It was hard to tell where the sound was coming from, but it was fairly close. My partner quietly motioned me to come around a corner. Then we heard the noise again. We were both poised to fire, but we stayed calm. Just then a box fell and something dashed out from behind it. It was a cat. The biggest, fattest short-haired cat I'd ever seen. Both my partner and I let out a long sigh of relief as we put our guns back in our holsters. The warehouse's resident mouse catcher had tripped the alarm. We had to laugh. Hey, I'm not ashamed to share some of the more ridiculous moments of my crazy life with you.

But seriously, if either of us had let fear get the better of us, we could have been shooting up the place and each other. Unfortunately, there have been instances where police officers have overreacted, with tragedy as the result. The best cops rarely if ever have to pull their trigger.

Fear of the unknown may be the scariest fear of all—am I right? It allows our imaginations to run wild with all sorts of over-the-top worst-case scenarios. This particular call turned out to be a false alarm, but there were others we responded to that weren't. That's why every situation had to be treated as if it was the "real thing," and certain protocols had to be followed. Process and procedures are your security blanket in potentially dangerous situations by keeping you focused and preventing you from overreacting.

Business sometimes is a pretty good reflection of the battlefield—it presents scary situations that can lead people to panic and overreact. When the stock market crashed a couple of years ago, Kayli, a friend of mine who has a marketing company, nearly went into a tailspin before she caught herself. A portion of her business capital was tied up in investments that all of a sudden were falling apart live on television and before her very eyes, within a matter of minutes. A six-hundred-point drop. Like that. It was serious.

I remember her telling me about it—the horrible churning feeling in her stomach, running to the bathroom to throw up (I'm sure a lot of people did the same thing that day), standing in front of the TV screen in her office stunned and silent.

"What could I do?" she told me. "I had to gather my thoughts; I couldn't sell anything off, that's for sure. And I couldn't panic, either, but I also really couldn't make client calls—I figured they'd be watching the TV, too, and probably didn't want to discuss branding."

Kayli did four things to deal with a very real situation, and I think they can be used as "protocol" for many kinds of frightening business situations—the loss of a job, client, or top employee; a shift in market conditions; a marketing or sales error; or a failure in leadership.

1. **Checked the facts:** Kayli called her investment adviser (she got through after about an hour of busy signals and leaving messages) and together they looked at how the market drop affected her investments and her business situation. Some of her investments were badly affected, others weren't.

2. **Decided on the right action:** In this case, Kayli decided to do nothing. She couldn't sell while the market was this volatile, and she wasn't going to add to her investments, either. She decided, correctly, as it turned out, to do nothing in terms of the market. She'd have to ride it out.

3. **Adjusted current and not-too-distant-future plans:** Kayli quickly checked upcoming events and projects— would she be able to see them through with the cash she had on hand? Would any need to be modified or canceled?

4. **Took a breather:** No sense hanging around the office waiting for the sky to fall some more. Kayli had done

what she could, made decisions, and adjusted what she could. Yet she also knew human nature and her own nature. She was still freaked by the day's events. Getting out of the office and removing herself from a situation she couldn't control was the best thing. And she was too distracted to do any serious work that day anyway. "I put on my running clothes and did three miles," she says. "The next day I felt a hell of a lot better and could focus on implementing the decisions I had made the day before."

Imagine if Kayli had not been afraid of what had happened to her investments that day. She wouldn't have looked at the facts, may not have made any short-term adjustments to her plans, might have called a client who was himself looking at his investments go down the drain—and maybe gotten a very unpleasant reception from him. Sometimes fear is good.

> Courage is not simply one of the virtues,
> but the form of every virtue at the testing point.
> —C. S. LEWIS

NAFOD, OR WHY FEAR IS A SIGN OF MENTAL HEALTH

During flight school I heard stories about guys being discharged or reassigned to desk jobs because of "NAFOD," an acronym often used by the Navy (less so by the Marines) that stands for No Apparent Fear Of Death. A landing-signal officer (a naval aviator who's trained to facilitate safe recovery of aircraft aboard aircraft carriers) pays close attention to student pilots who don't seem to have any personal limits or sense of danger and "grades" them as NAFOD—which is not considered a good thing. Those are the guys you have to worry about because they're the most prone to take really ridiculous chances that can put themselves and others in harm's way.

> **Combat Confidence:** Certain fears are a normal and healthy reaction to a real or imminent danger.

All branches of the military realize that some level of fear is required because it encourages calculation before action, safe practices, and consideration for comrades, civilians, and equipment. No branch of the military would have any use for a reckless person who may endanger their lives or livelihood, not to mention those of other people. Nor for that matter would a corporate boss or banker who gives small business loans. Some level of fear is *required* for good decision making. Don't get down on yourself for feeling afraid, because it's real—and often legit. I'd be a lot more concerned for your safety and chances for success if you were completely *without* fear.

I know it sounds counterintuitive to the Zero to Breakthrough mentality: "Vernice, I thought you were going to help me get over my fear of [fill in the blank], not acquiesce to it." But it's not. Sometimes our red flags wave for a reason, and we should pay attention to them.

Think back to the 2010 Vancouver winter Olympics. Do you remember that the Dutch men's bobsledding team pulled out of the competition at the last minute? Bobsledding is a fast and dangerous sport where teams of two or four make a series of timed runs down narrow, twisting, banked iced tracks in gravity-powered sleds. You might also recall that Nodar Kumaritashvili, a twenty-one-year-old Georgian luge slider competing at the same Olympics, died after crashing and hitting a metal pole during a training run. Kumaritashvili told his father that he was "terrified" of the track—the same one he crashed and died on.

Although Dutch bobsledder Edwin van Calker said the luger's death had nothing to do with van Calker's decision to quit, the sled driver told his coach he couldn't drive the track because he, like Nodar, "was terrified." Van Calker had already crashed on his first run during a two-man practice on Saturday, as did seven other sleds on that same day and on the same track. Those accidents and his memory of previous crashes, including one that put two of his teammates in the hospital, hung heavily in his heart and mind. It came down to surviving, not performing for the crowds. "I have to look after my boys and can't close my eyes to that," he told reporters.

His coach, Tom De La Hunty, told reporters that he'd never before seen an athlete refuse to compete at a major event because he was scared. "You keep your inner fears to yourself and do it," he said at a news conference. "That's why it's such a popular sport in the military. It's that kind of macho sport. You go over the top together."

Despite these comments, the coach supported van Calker's decision to call it quits. It seemed like the right decision to me. He might have done the run without incidence. But he recognized that this was no ordinary fear—it felt tangible and visceral. When you're that scared, the right choice is to walk away. In the case of the bobsledder, for example, his driving ability may have been drastically compromised *because* of what he was feeling, with potentially deadly consequences.

When you are experiencing intense anxiety, it's time to go with your gut. Part of instinctual thinking and intuitive decision making, which I talked about in Chapter 3, is in knowing when *not* to go forward. If you're smart enough to know how to do something, then you're also savvy enough to know when to stop, step back, or take a break. It's not failure if the benefits of not doing something outweigh the advantages of doing it. Hey, you can always try again later.

Say you know your company is going through some tough times, and you know there will be layoffs at the end of the quarter. Maybe you should be a little scared of that. So put off that vacation until after you know what's going to happen. Why? Well . . . you might be one of the unlucky ones who are laid off. You'll need that vacation money for rent (you have to be pragmatic, not unrealistic or fatalistic, when it comes to fears). Besides, this is not the time to give the boss any ideas, even if they're false, about you being a goof-off. Sit tight, keep your head down, and let the fear motivate you to show what a valuable person you are. Even if you do end up getting laid off, you have a better chance of leaving with a great recommendation from your boss. Listen, I'm not trying to scare you, but the reality is that if you have reason to be scared of anything—a career shift, a new colleague who seems sort of threatening, or a sticky situation with an unhappy employee, you have to recognize that you're not just pulling the fear factor out of your hat. It's real.

Here are a few breakthrough tips for having the courage to face your fears, wherever you find them:

- *Tell someone about your fear when appropriate.* I disagree with coach De La Hunty that you should always keep fears to yourself. Okay, exposing your fears to people who don't have your best interests at heart is a bad idea (your competitor will use it against you) or to those who are under your supervision (like your children or employees, for example) because it may cause them to panic. However, I do think sharing your fears with those you trust can alleviate some of the pain that's involved in keeping the fear a secret. It really depends on the circumstances.

  During my sophomore year in college, I discovered through a self-exam that I had a cyst on my right breast. I can tell you, I was really terrified. I knew I needed to see the doctor. As soon as I shared the news with friends I felt free because I knew that they were holding that information for me. They had taken up some of the burden of it simply because they knew about it. That's where your wingmen really come in handy—they can carry some of the fear for you, but only if you tell them about it.

- *Follow your fear if it means doing otherwise would put everything you have at risk.* Taking a calculated risk means weighing the costs and benefits to an activity. Say you're afraid to walk into a networking event where you don't know anyone. This is a common fear, and not especially irrational. Do a cost-benefit analysis of walking into that room. If everyone ignores you, will you be ruined financially, emotionally, or physically? If not, go for it. However, if you're considering spending all your savings to go to a networking event halfway across the world where you don't know anyone, the trip might not be worth the investment. Stay home. Investing your own money in a business? Only do it if you can survive if the business fails.

- *Avoid following through on fears that put others at unwanted or unnecessary risk.* If you're scared that someone might get hurt (including yourself) on any level, think again. Never knowingly put yourself or others at risk of physical, financial, or emotional harm. Likewise, if you can't change the outcome or get another crack at something if you fail, and a failed result can't be undone, your fear is likely based on reality. If something requires you to do it before you can evaluate the pros and cons, again, your fears may be well-founded.

Be thankful that most of the fears we have aren't a reaction to actual physical danger. Believe me, living with that kind of anxiety on a daily basis is not fun. In fact, you probably take a lot of fear in stride without thinking too much about it. For instance, how many times have you been sitting at your desk viciously knocking down e-mails when all of a sudden an adversary pops up right in front of you? "Meeting in ten minutes!" "Can you step into my office?" *Shoot. What now?* Or have you ever been driving down the highway when out of nowhere an ice storm or rainstorm blows in and you are faced with a set of unexpected driving hazards? If you have found yourself in either of these situations, you most likely sat up straight, braced yourself, and reengaged with the new threat—all within seconds. Now you recognize that you have the natural skills to face your fears and can utilize them when put in a scary situation.

So why are there so many things we're afraid to do or dread facing? We all have different dispositions. There are people who will never get on a roller coaster—you can be a success in life without doing so. But there are other things we don't do out of fear that hold us back. Those are the activities that are directly related to fulfilling our dreams and following our passions.

When I ask audiences and groups about their common anxieties, what I usually hear is a handy excuse to avoid situations that they believe will make them look unprepared or feel inadequate and humiliated. That kind of fear can easily become a habit—an automatic reaction to any uncomfortable, unfamiliar circumstance. Sure, by bowing out of anything risky you might not ever be embarrassed, but you'll also never have a breakthrough. "Comfortable" is not what you're going for when you're going from Zero to Breakthrough.

The fears that keep you from trying something new, asking for what you need, or testing the limits of your knowledge are directly correlated to:

1. Not knowing what is going to happen, or "what if" syndrome.
2. Not taking or having the time to review the pros and cons of doing whatever it is you're afraid to do. You feel pressured to act when you still feel unsure.
3. The possibility of experiencing unpleasantness, pain, and/or failure.

Combat Confidence: Use fear to your advantage by looking at it as a field guide to the areas of your life in which you need to acquire more knowledge.

When I first started my speaking career, I had all sorts of anxiety-based reservations: "What if I'm boring," "Maybe

I don't have much to say," and "Will anyone actually pay to hear me?" Turns out most public speakers have these fears, and they're natural and perfectly fine as long as they don't interfere with the goal of public speaking. See, this is where it gets tricky. Self-doubt and anxiety about the unknown didn't stop me—but they often paralyze other people from trying something new. A breakthrough mentality stops fear or anxiety from getting the better of you. As long as you're conscious of what you're afraid of, breakthrough mentality can beat it back.

Acknowledge the Fear

This is a huge first step. If this is all you do today, you've accomplished something major. Too many of us put off unpacking the anxiety suitcase. Put your fears down in your journal, write them on a napkin, or take a piece of sidewalk chalk and scrawl them on your driveway. Putting a fear in writing externalizes it—you can literally look at what you're anxious about. At that point you can honestly assess how big and bad it is. Once you have stopped giving the fears power over your actions and ambitions, you can cross them out, throw them away, or hose 'em off the driveway. Feels pretty good, doesn't it?

Feel the Fear—and Go with It

Once you've put your fears "out there," feel them. Prediction: It won't be nearly as bad as you think. Even if it is, so what? You're still here, right? One of the reasons why we don't want to face our fears is because it's going to be painful. You just have to be ready to tolerate more emotional pain and physical exhaustion than you thought you could. But you can. The more you feel the fear/pain, the smaller it gets and the higher your tolerance becomes until finally the fear/pain is—*poof*—gone. Fear, anxiety, self-doubt, and worry are all part of life. Avoidance only creates a tougher fear that's harder to conquer.

One of the best ways I have found to get over a fear is to practice whatever it is I'm afraid of. When I joined the ROTC I had a fear that I would not be able to keep up with the strenuous drills and be able to pass the physical fitness test. I figured I needed to actually start doing it before I even got to the drill field. So I started running every day. I created and completed my own physical fitness test every Friday. When the real one came up it wasn't all that scary.

Combat Confidence: Respond; don't react.

Reacting to scary situations comes from emotion (see Chapter 2); it's often illogical and disorganized and can have negative results. Responding appropriately, with quick thinking and confidence, is logical and feeling-neutral and usually has positive results.

Scared of speaking in public? Speak in public. Get a group of your BTBs (Breakthrough Buddies) together and give them a talk on something you know about—even if it's baking apple pie. Afraid to ask your boss for a raise? Ask someone else, a friend or family member, for a raise first. Ask them to answer you with a "no" every time you ask so you get used to hearing it, because no is what you're probably afraid of. Or maybe you're afraid he'll say yes and give you more work to do, and you won't be able to handle it. Okay, then have your friend say, "Sure, you've got yourself a raise, along with some extra responsibilities." After you go through a few mock Q&As, your apprehensions will dissipate—seriously. The real thing? Piece of cake!

What's the Worst That Could Happen?

As you review your fears, look at them with a cold, logical eye, and ask yourself, "What's the worst that could happen if I follow through with [fill in the blank]?" You learn a lot about both your fear and the action it stems from. When I started to think about the speaking business, I grappled with the idea of speaking only in front of women rather than giving talks and workshops in front of mixed audiences. As I considered the various options, I asked myself, "What's the worst that could happen?"

Well, there may be less of a market and less money if I limit myself to women-only groups. I also might have to limit my topics. What would be the worst thing about that? Maybe I wouldn't have enough money to pay my bills in the beginning, or maybe not for a long time. What's the worst thing that could happen then? My business might fail, and I would no longer be living my purpose. The process led me to an essential question: What are the minimum requirements for me to be able to both live and live my purpose?

I looked at my current situation and saw that limiting myself to the women's market could be devastating to long-term goals. I also faced the fear that men would not be interested in what I had to say. I realized that was a ridiculous idea. Today, I speak to all sorts of groups—small and large, female only and mostly male, half men and half women, young and old.

> Every time we choose safety, we reinforce fear.
>
> —CHERI HUBER, ZEN TEACHER

Prepare Yourself for Battle

In *The Survivor's Club*, journalist Ben Sherwood reported that only 10 percent of the population would be able to take immediate, positive action in response to an emergency situation. A whopping 80 percent of us either would be stuck like the proverbial deer caught in the headlights and do nothing or simply run as fast as we could—that's our fight or flight instinct. The remaining 10 percent would react negatively, act out, and hurt either themselves or others or both. According to Sherwood, 90 percent of us don't know self-preservation techniques or how to use them, even when push comes to shove.

What makes the 10 percent who know what to do different from the rest of us? Sherwood says that this group naturally strategizes a plan of action for most situations before something happens. For example, when they get on an airplane they immediately scope out the exits and devise an escape plan. This plan gives a sense of structure, which in turn creates a sense of calm. This is certainly true of military men and women—we're trained to create a battle plan before stepping into enemy territory.

We have contingencies, which I've talked about in the previous chapters, and we are trained to think intuitively. Both these skills allow you to face and prepare for the unknown. Although everyday situations are not emergency-based, it does point out the need to be responsive instead of reactive in our daily life. It's a good habit to have—when you catch yourself saying "what if," answer! What would you do *if* . . . the boss turned you down for a raise, the sales conference presentation wasn't a success, the charity event you planned didn't raise enough money?

Second, it's very helpful to find someone like you who overcame the same fear and find out how they did it, either by studying that person if they are not available to you or by asking them if they are. You might find yourself asking what to do if there isn't anyone like you who did what you want to do. It so happens I was in that situation. There had been one or two black women who had tried to become Marine pilots, but they didn't make it. There was no way I was going to take their baggage on my trip, as in, "Oh, she didn't do it, so what makes me think I can?"

So what I did was look at the people who *had* become pilots, white guys, black guys, whoever, and I asked myself: What is the difference between these guys and me, once you eliminate gender and color? That's the package—how about the stuff inside? Once I looked at it that way, I knew that if a white guy could do it, so could a black woman (me). After that I had no doubt I was capable of operating a Cobra. It never crossed my mind that I could fail.

Practice Mental Toughness

I've always thought of myself as an emotionally strong person. Maybe it's my determination, or that I'm an optimist by nature. When I joined the Marines, I got the equivalent of a PhD in mental toughness. The Marines train you—through trial and fire—to sharpen your psychological and physiological edge so that you can consistently handle high-pressure situations with confidence, knowledge, and focus. In other words, we learn how to perform at maximum potential *all the time.*

Mental toughness has some awesome advantages. It enables us to:

- Dive into nasty circumstances with full force and confidence.

- Do whatever it takes to get the job done.

- Excel not despite, but *because of,* high pressure and unpredictable situations.

- Bounce back quickly after a setback, and jump right back in.

- Produce results even if the likelihood of success is low.

- Remain unshakable through painful, grueling, or stressful situations.

I know, I know—you want to get yourself some of that. Mental toughness is a skill you can learn, although it's easier for some people than for others. The obstacle is that most of us are motivated more by pleasure than by pain. Just look at dieting—most people who are overweight find it very difficult to reduce and keep the pounds off over the long term. Losing weight is hard because the pain of deprivation just isn't very appealing over months and years. The pleasure of the taste and smell of delicious food, along with the social aspects of eating without having to think about every ounce and calorie, is much more enticing. The breakthrough occurs when it becomes more painful to be overweight than it is to not have the food. Then dieting "suddenly" doesn't seem as difficult as it used to be.

On some level it's human nature to want an outcome without having to do the work it takes to get there. There's always stress surrounding the setting of long-term goals (building a new business, working toward earning a series of promotions over time) as opposed to immediate gratification (keep getting the paycheck at your current job, working to maintain the status quo). At some point you have to ask yourself what's more important, achieving a goal or being satisfied with how things are now?

Marines develop mental toughness as recruit officer candidates. We go through an eleven-station obstacle course called the Confidence Course, which helps us build mental and physical strength. I'm not going to go into great detail about what happens in the course. A few highlights should give you a pretty good idea of how the Marines separate the strong from the weak (not everyone makes it through).

Combat Confidence: If you say you can't or think you can't, you definitely can't. If you say you can or think you can, you might! It's like breaking the four-minute-mile record—for years no one thought a mile could be run in less than four minutes. So naturally the perceived wisdom had it that it was impossible to run a mile in less than four minutes. Then, what do you know, Australian John Walker (ironic, isn't it?) became the first person to run a mile in under 3.5 minutes. All of a sudden quite a few other people started running a mile in less than four minutes, too.

During the third week of training, anxious recruits leave their squads and file into a Weapons and Field Training classroom to wait for one of the most feared aspects of training: the Gas Chamber. They've heard about this part of the test from Marines and read about it on the Internet. In the classroom the recruits learn how to use a gas mask properly so it can save their lives in an environment with a potentially hazardous substance. Once you are confident that you know how to use the mask, you go into a gas chamber.

The gas used in the Gas Chamber is chlorobenzylidene malonitrile, or CS gas, a nonlethal substance that is used in all branches of the military and police departments as a riot control agent. Each recruit spends about three to five minutes in the chamber—depending on how long he or she can stand it. These probably are the longest minutes of their lives up to this moment. I had already gone through this training in the

Army, so I knew what to expect, and I was fine. Once the gas has filled the chamber, the future Marines are told to remove their masks and put them on top of their heads. At this point there always are some recruits who start to panic. Despite mental preparation, your body reacts: you tear, your nose runs, and you do tend to panic, even if it's momentarily. It's tough to stay the course when your body is fighting to flee.

Fortunately for most of us, our daily challenges don't require stepping into an actual gas chamber. But I use this story as a way of showing that all of us can fight panic and fear. We can develop persistence, grit, staying power, and grace under pressure by doing things we don't want to do, don't like to do, are afraid to do, or think we can't do—your own version of the Confidence Course. You've heard the expression "go the extra mile"—participating above and beyond the minimum requirements of any activity or obligation. The practice of doing more than you have to do builds mental toughness, especially when it involves something that is physically challenging or psychologically and emotionally difficult.

How about public speaking—it was something I was afraid to do when I started, and now I do it for a living. But I know there are a lot of people who think getting up in front of even a handful of people and giving a pitch or a presentation is like going into a gas chamber. If that's you, I've got news. You've got to start getting up in front of people as often as possible and start yakking. And you've got to project confidence and make what you're saying sound interesting. Every businessperson at some point has to make his or her case in front of others. Get used to it.

The same goes for people who are afraid to fly. If your business or job doesn't require any travel, then you might be able to get away with not getting on an airplane. But if by avoiding flights you're damaging your chances to win new clients, work on career-enhancing projects, or network with people who could be beneficial to your work, then you've got to start flying. And as often as possible.

So what are you afraid of that is also holding you back from your breakthrough? Think about it, identify it, and do it tomorrow.

BREAK POINT CASE STUDY: VERNICE'S BIG IRAQ ADVENTURE

I'll never forget the first time I flew into enemy territory with my partner Ruvalcaba. It was nighttime, and we were heading into the northwest of Basra against a deathly black sky; the dim light of the moon just barely illuminated a haunting picture of what had occurred earlier in the day. Hundreds of oil fires had been set and numerous battles fought on the ground. Vehicles, some American, most Iraqi, smoldered below like the last dying embers in a charcoal pit. By now the smoke from the oil fires had risen to our flying altitude, creating an eerie haze all around us.

As we drew closer to the Iraqi border, I followed our progress on the map to ensure that we stayed on course. It was so quiet I could almost hear my heart beat. As I scanned the ground, I could see the rickety metal fence that divided not only two countries but also two worlds.

You may have seen war movies where a character says, "We're three clicks away from the target," one click being one thousand kilometers, as they zero in on a location. That's an authentic depiction of military lingo. I counted down three clicks, two clicks, one click . . . we had crossed the border and were in enemy territory. Once we crossed over, we still had no communication with the guys on the ground. I could feel my body armor underneath my seat. What if we get shot down? This was no cardboard target simulation exercise. This was a living, breathing enemy that could shoot back and kill me. And that was their sole intent.

After all, a ground missile could come at us at any moment. Raw fear started to take over my emotions, and I could feel myself almost physically pushing it away. I was terrified. It was humbling for me to realize that despite the fact that I was well trained for my mission and in control of a fierce fighting machine, I could tangibly feel the fear. Was my partner scared, too? Maybe he was fine. I decided not to focus on my fear and relied on my training. I was prepared for this moment.

There were no casualties on my first flight into hostile territory, but it was an extreme situation filled with unknowns and the possibility of danger, destruction, violence, and death. Without opening a can of worms, let's say that the insurgents' rules of engagement were different from ours, and their methods of fighting were unpredictable at best.

I called on the higher power that my father talked to me about. "Faith doesn't eliminate fear, but it gives you someplace to put it," he'd say whenever I doubted myself. A lot of the pressure is released when you know that something bigger than you is holding your fear while you redirect your energy toward positive action.

At this moment, I focused on what we were there to do—monitor and communicate with other aircraft that were flying with us and keep the ground troops safe. The job at hand stopped me from obsessing over the dreadful and very real possibilities. I was able to harness that "fear energy" to stay calm and focused. What good was being consumed with thoughts of being shot down to my comrades or myself anyway?

Imagine the red glow from a high-powered laser burning through a piece of granite. That's how I felt as I searched the terrain below for anything that might put us in danger. It was all clear. Mission accomplished. We had flown into enemy territory and made it safely back out, as did our fellow Marines and their aircraft. In the days to come we would not always be so lucky. But on this day, as we crossed back over that small gray "world divider," I let out a sigh of relief. After we landed back at base, I reflected on the emotions I had experienced and the actions I had taken to stay connected to my team and to my mission:

1. **Acknowledged I was scared:** Sometimes just saying to yourself, "This is some scary s$%!, that's happening," provides relief—if only for enough time to regain your composure and get back to the fight.

2. **Gave the fear to my higher power:** Doing so made it a heck of a lot easier to do my job. Let God worry about it for now.

3. **Responded:** I reminded myself there were Marines on the ground who needed our support, and acted accordingly.

4. **Chose the outcome I wanted but was ready to accept and deal with any outcome I got:** My objective: the safe return of the troops I was looking out for. Marines don't leave Marines behind. Hard as it was in this circumstance, I also had to stay open to other outcomes and see the value in, well, whatever happened.

BREAK POINT CASE STUDY:
CLIMBING THE MOUNTAIN OF FEAR

As someone who has experienced the thrill, the pain, and the complexities of being a professional athlete, I have both an admiration and appreciation for women who tackle sports traditionally thought of as men-only activities. Katie Brown is one such woman. She's a small-framed, delicate twenty-nine-year-old with the power of a lioness. At age thirteen she began sport climbing in her home state of Kentucky. She developed into a fierce "difficulty climber," won the X Games and a climbing World Cup, completed a free climb (without prior knowledge of the route) of the northwest face of Yosemite's Half Dome, and has scaled mountains all over the world, including Europe, Asia, and India.

In her very inspiring book *Girl on the Rocks*, Katie calls the twinge of fear a climber feels when she is parallel to a vertical rock so empowering that you want to experience the sensation again and again. True, the exhilaration of fear can be addictive, especially to daredevils and tomboys.

Katie gets an adrenaline rush from feeling scared. But when she was about twenty, she wanted to take some time off from the sport. After seven straight years of full-time devotion to climbing, she needed to plant her feet on the ground and do something different. Two years later, she decided to get back into the sport she had cherished. "I loved climbing again because I found a renewed passion, motivation, and pure enjoyment for it," she recalled. "But I also hated it because for some reason I found myself inexplicably scared of falling—so scared in fact that I would freeze and be unable to move."

Katie became so frustrated with herself that she would cry and agonize over her "failings" at not being able to mount rocks that in the past she scampered up like a puppy dog on a grassy mound. It may have been that as an adult climber, she understood the consequences of a climb gone wrong, whereas when she was younger her innocence protected her from this fear. She still went ahead and did a climb, and then another and another, and over time the fear lessened—although it's always in the background.

There are five key tactics Katie uses to overcome her fear of climbing, and she uses them well before she puts climbing boot to rock. "It's best to start the overcoming process before leaving the ground," she says. If you wait until you're completely paralyzed with fear, it's too late. Affirmations, or positive self-talk, helped Katie realize that even if she did fall, nothing would happen: "The rope is going to catch you." Conscious, deep, slow breathing reserves strength and helps to prevent hyper-ventilation, which can come on when you're panicked. Shallow breathing is tiring and leads to more anxiety.

Visualization helped Katie successfully climb a mountain in her mind. In doing so, she could look fear in the eye, and tell it to go away! One of my favorites—and you're going to have to find a safe place to do this—is to scream. That's right. Let out your best glass-shattering, blood-curdling horror-movie scream either before you are about to do something scary or while something scary (like falling) is happening.

"It's a great release—a way of expelling the fear as I let go," she says. Katie also makes a conscious effort to step out of her comfort zone regularly: "If you don't ever push yourself, you'll never conquer your fears." Katie says that eventually she notices her comfort zone has expanded. Finally, and I have to say that this really caught my attention, Katie uses what she calls chick power. "Don't be afraid to use the desire to impress those watching you to your advantage."

Katie's tactics can be used by anyone facing a scary situation, whether it's getting up the courage to ask for more responsibility and money at your job, going head to head with a competitor, dealing with the unpleasant task of firing an unsatisfactory employee, or breaking up with a mate. Let's look at what Katie did:

1. **Decided the outcome was going to be what she wanted it to be—safe and positive:** For Katie it was making it up the mountain without falling, not panicking, and continuing to climb if she did fall.

2. **Recognized the scary feeling but went ahead with the plan anyway:** Katie admitted to herself that she was scared, but she didn't let it stop her.

3. **Got the fear out of her system:** Scream! Airpower! Hooah! Whatever you call a loud shout—I love it. If you can't yell (they might not like it down at the office), can you go into the restroom and do fifteen jumping jacks, go for a run, or head for the gym and don boxing gloves and work the punching bag over? Physical activity helps you get rid of the nervous energy fear engenders.

4. **Saw herself doing it:** Katie saw herself tackle the mountain. Can you, in your mind's eye, walk yourself through asking for the raise, breaking up with Mr. or Ms. Wrong, or winning the race? See yourself doing it often enough, and doing whatever it is you have to do becomes more familiar and comfortable.

5. **Used her ego for strength:** Any landing pad in a storm will do! If your pride and self-image give you the guts to go forward, I'm all for it. In Katie's case, a desire to impress the other climbers with her skill and agility gave her the nerve she needed to climb higher.

Z2B EXERCISE: STRETCH YOUR COMFORT ZONE

Like climber Katie Brown says, the more you stretch yourself, even in small ways, the more you expand what you feel comfortable doing. Do one thing today that is *uncomfortable*. For a shy person it might be talking to the person next to them at the bus station or on line for coffee. For the person trying to lose weight, picking a favorite food to eliminate can demonstrate not only courage and willpower but assure them they have the strength to do what's good for their waistline, even if it hurts. The manager who is afraid his or her people can't handle crucial responsibilities can give them an important task *today* and see what happens. Give them the proper oversight along with the materials and information they need to succeed, but without micromanaging. What happened? What went right? What could have gone better? How can you stretch yourself tomorrow?

Z2B EXERCISE: TRANSFER YOUR CONFIDENCE

Take a few minutes of quiet time in the car or on the bus on your way to work or school, while you're grocery shopping, in the morning before you get up, or in the evening when you're ready for bed. Think back to the times in life when you felt self-assured. What were the circumstances? Remember in as much detail as possible. What was the common denominator? My own confidence always stems from being and feeling prepared and ready. Is it the same for you? How does the activity that motivated you to be prepared compare to the thing you fear now? Are there components that are similar?

For example, I felt confident as a runner and a football player—but the Marines swimming test? That freaked me out. Running on the firm earth, that I could handle. I could even handle some strong women coming at me with a very strong desire to knock me down. Looking at the situation logically, I could see that swimming, like playing an earthbound sport, was an intense physical challenge. Like running, it required stamina. In fact, there was a lot about the swimming test that was similar to other sports challenges I had met successfully. Once I figured this out, I could transfer the feeling of confidence I had about playing football to my swimming practice and test. It worked.

Combat Confidence: The opposite of fear is faith. Believe in God or your higher power, believe in what you know, believe in your wingmen and Breakthrough Buddies, and believe in yourself.

WHAT WOULD CHESTY DO?

At the start of this chapter you read a famous quote attributed to Lieutenant General Lewis Burwell "Chesty" Puller, a Marine Corp folk hero and the most highly decorated Marine in history. No question, he was a badass military commander in the best sense of the word—admired by his men and feared by his adversaries. Unlike other officers, Puller was known and loved for his willingness to get his hands dirty—he fought in the trenches alongside his troops and never winced or shuddered in battle, even when under the most unrelenting and dangerous fire. He had complete faith in his troops and they in him. That shared respect made them strong both as a group and as individuals.

Puller was inspiringly brave—one story has it that when a grenade landed next to him, he looked at it and calmly pronounced it "a dud" while everyone around him dove for cover (he was right). He was also fair-minded—one time Chesty noticed a second lieutenant order an enlisted man to salute him one hundred times for missing a salute. "You were absolutely correct in making him salute you one hundred times, Lieutenant," he said, and added, "but you know that an officer must return every salute he receives. Now return them all."

That fearless, win-at-all-costs attitude won him fourteen medals for combat bravery and the undying admiration of Marines to this day. In fact, a common boot camp chant at the end of a tough day is "Good night, Chesty Puller, wherever you are!" Just thinking about Puller's example can make a shaky Marine feel heroic. There's something to that—your bravery in the face of adversity has a positive impact on the people around you. It's an example of what Marines call esprit de corps, or a sense of group pride. A lot of times it's easier to be brave for others than it is to be brave for yourself. Who needs you to be strong? Who has faith in you? Take that faith and turn it into personal strength. Channel your "inner Chesty" for them— and keep forging ahead.

FLY-AWAYS

- Fear is okay; don't be ashamed of it.

- Don't let fear be an excuse for inaction.

- Acknowledge your fear and deal with it head-on.

- Respond to fear; don't react to it.

- Be ready for the unknown by preparing for "what if" situations.

- Develop your mental toughness muscle.

- If you can't be brave for yourself, be brave for someone (or something) you care about.

CHAPTER 6

You've Arrived, Now Keep Going: Flight and Future

Expect something wonderful . . . claim it.

—GASTON ARMOUR, OFFICER, GENTLEMAN, AND MY FATHER

We were in a remote town in the middle of Iraq and it was pitch-black. But that wasn't any excuse. I had to find the target so we could use our Global Positioning System (GPS) for more accurate targeting. The target would be a house that sat next to a fenced-in two-story building that had a mural of Saddam Hussein painted on it. Finally the controller on the ground was able to give us the grid coordinates.

There was an urgency to find the target because our missile was going to be the signal for the start of the raid on the house, which contained a high-priority target. Because raids ideally have an element of surprise, the house couldn't be marked with smoke or flares. We were strictly limited to visual identification.

As we circled, I continued scanning. Then I found it. I used our laser pointer to highlight the building for the pilot in the back. Once he saw it, he moved the aircraft into position to fire the missile.

The troops on the ground were in position and ready to move. My heart felt like it was going to explode, it was racing so fast. The rush of adrenaline and intensity gave me a high that's difficult to put into words. Once the missile was in range, I pulled the trigger and guided it to the target. There was an explosion as we pulled away. The Marines moved in and we supported the rest of the raid from overhead, always in position if the ground troops needed air support. At the end of the night, the mission had been accomplished successfully.

During another attack to destroy Iraqi antiaircraft artillery, I spotted enemy fire. Major Ruvalcaba pulled the aircraft off in one direction as I kept shooting to the left until we were out of range of their artillery. As we made another pass, I could see the Fedayeen troops below, so Ruvalcaba fired more rockets. The Fedayeen Saddam (Saddam's Men of Sacrifice) was founded by Saddam Hussein's son Uday in 1995. This "army"—actually a vicious security force that protected Saddam and his family—had anywhere between 18,000 and 40,000 troops, mostly poor young men recruited from regions loyal to Saddam. They definitely seemed to have NAFOD (No Apparent Fear Of Death) down pat.

At this point it seemed to us that Fedayeen were falling to the ground, but at first we couldn't tell if they were going down because they had been shot and wounded or killed, or because they were taking cover in an attempt to deceive and then attack us. Seeing them use this strategy before was like a real-life version of a horror movie where the monster has been "killed," only to get up and start attacking as soon as the star turns his or her back and breathes a sigh of relief. I couldn't turn my back on any portion of the battlefield. If the enemy isn't dead he *always* tries to creep back in. So you have to kill him before he kills you.

There was no movement, no fire from below, so we believed we had subdued the ground troops. Good. Each time I destroyed one of my targets—military tank, ammunition site—I felt a tremendous sense of accomplishment, of protecting our troops who otherwise would have walked into an ambush.

As a Marine and now as a civilian, my question after any "mission accomplished" is always, *what next?* Or, as Yogi Berra said, "It ain't over til it's over." During this mission, we weren't ready to go back to base. We had to move forward to protect one of our convoys, and that's when my weapons system went berserk. In the military you learn very quickly that one success doesn't automatically translate into subsequent successes. The more you do the better you get, but there are always elements you can't predict or control. In this case, it turned out all right; we were able to deal. And I never let my successes on the battle-field raise my expectations about the next mission. You never know . . . you just have to go.

SUCCESS INERTIA

Success is not a single destination where, upon arrival, you stop, game over. You didn't think it would be, did you? The way I see it, accomplishments come with responsibility; break-throughs require commitment. The responsibility is to build on past achievements by establishing fresh goals and meeting new challenges; the commitment is to continue trying even when one breakthrough isn't immediately followed by another.

Microsoft founder Bill Gates frequently talks about the success spiral, where you always work toward building one success on another, and then another. This doesn't mean missteps along the way are a repudiation of what you've accomplished or a predictor of what you'll achieve in the future. It just means you have to keep going and try again.

> **Combat Confidence:** You're off the ground now, so keep rising. Mediocrity was never your dream.

Unfortunately, I've met many people who are frightened off by a big success. For some it's because they believe they won't be able to live up to it, so they don't even try. They go into a failure spiral. And there are companies that hit it big with an idea or a product but can't replicate it because managers and employees spend too much time resting on their laurels, depending on that win to maintain their position as top dog. Or they keep doing the same things over and over again, refusing to go in a new direction, even if they see the market changing. By the time they decide to do something about it, it's too late; they are just too far behind the curve. I call this success inertia—where you give your victory so much juice your brakes get flooded and you can't go anywhere else.

There's a guy I know, a medical researcher I'll call Bob, who was a leader on a team that developed a cutting-edge process for separating and identifying antibodies in cells. Bob's contribution to the discovery was both a scientific and a personal breakthrough. He was rewarded handsomely for his work, spoke at conferences, and became regarded as a "wunderkind" within the antibody research community. Over time, after the accolades and awards were collected, the admiring smiles and high-fives disappeared. Bob was left to guide his team to another discovery.

Some minor insights were gained along the way, but nothing that advanced the lab in any significant way. Bob felt as if his team was counting on him, and he couldn't deliver. Bob had inertia; he called it "winner's block." He could not get that first hit out of his mind. The pressure was claustrophobic. Slowly his team moved on to new projects and formed new groups. After a while Bob went back to routine research and faded into the background at his company. "That Bob," he imagined his colleagues saying, "we thought he was really going to be something." It may have been even worse—his colleagues probably didn't think about him at all.

There are so many examples of success inertia in the business world that you can take your pick. Internet service AOL comes to mind. They famously allowed their successful existing businesses (Netscape, for example) to go by the wayside while they tried unsuccessfully to take on new, younger, more agile competitors in emerging markets that they didn't understand. They lost market share in their successful businesses, along with that all-important "hip factor" that savvy tech consumers expect, which really tarnished what was once a very strong brand.

Classic business school examples come from Firestone,

which was the gold standard for tires in the United States at the end of the 1960s. French competitor Michelin then introduced a superior radial tire, which consumers and carmakers began to favor over Firestone's bias tire. Even though Firestone knew about radials, they kept producing the bias tire, perhaps feeling that their brand was unbeatable. Ultimately they fell into financial distress and eventually they had to go on the block. Bridgestone, a Japanese company, bought the firm.

I'm not into frilly dresses (or is that obvious?), but British manufacturer Laura Ashley was, especially throughout the 1960s and 1970s. They had a huge impact on fashion, and ladies and little girls alike loved the company's cotton flowered peasant dresses. When women started to enter the workforce in great numbers during the late 1970s, ruffles and daisies just were not going to cut it on Wall Street. Even though demand for its dresses decreased, Laura Ashley's management hesitated to adjust the company's brand image to include work-friendly outfits. That inertia proved to be a huge financial blow: The company entered a decade-long period of red ink before reestablishing itself—although not at the level they once were.

Clearly, success inertia can be costly. How do you prevent this from happening to you or your company? How do you keep charging toward the next big thing? First of all, get the notion that all great victories have to be followed by even more monumental achievements out of your head. I can tell you from experience that flops and misses are part and parcel of even those who seemingly have the Midas touch. You just never remember them because successful people and companies don't let their successes lull them into a false sense of security, and they never allow failures to defeat them.

When you are pursuing your passion and fulfilling your life's purpose, breakthroughs are very much like the cycle of life. There are times when breakthroughs are bursting forth in great succession—like hundreds of roses blooming on a single bush in late spring. At other times, you can have two or three breakthroughs over a longer stretch of time. Of course, there will be rest periods and downtime, useful for refueling, thinking, and planning. A lot happens during these dormant periods.

To be truly effective at not falling prey to success inertia, you have to be conscious of your surroundings and feelings. At the end of this chapter, I will have you write about what it feels like to have a breakthrough. Be prepared: Not all of your feelings will be positive. That's completely normal. Think about this: As a member of the Marine Corps, I took human lives. Taking out the enemy was one of the definitions of success as a soldier. When I joined the Army and Marine Corps, I knew what I was signing up for. I joined an organization that trains soldiers to take lives during war, and in the name of national security. I don't apologize for it, but I never took the responsibility lightly. I'm immensely proud of having been able to serve my country and thankful for having joined the Corps.

To keep on flying high and build on your breakthroughs, keep these strategies in mind:

Take a Break, But Keep It Short

Give yourself a pat on the back and feel appreciated. Savor your success. You can take a furlough if you want to—if you've completed a grueling phase of your project or finished something that required a great deal of physical energy, rest is essential. Just don't let it extend for more than a week or two. Yes, you deserve a vacation, but if you let your furlough go on for too long, momentum will be lost and it can take time to get back in the groove.

> We are what we repeatedly do.
> Excellence then, is not an act, but a habit.
> —ARISTOTLE

Analyze the Process So You Can Strategically Duplicate Success

We've already talked about how important it is to learn from failures and criticism. Success is a teacher, too. At a recent Raytheon Finance Leadership Conference, the company's chairman, Michael Ruettgers, spoke. The Raytheon company had developed a new missile guidance system, and when they tested it, it hit the target the first time—right out of the gate. The other two test missiles didn't work as well.

Okay, maybe that first try was a fluke and the missiles really didn't work. Maybe a failure would tell the real story. Ruettgers said this would be taking a negative outcome at face value and a positive one as an accident—but maybe it was the other way around. So they went back and analyzed the first success to see why that launch worked so perfectly, and they discovered that it wasn't just dumb luck. There were factors unique to that first exercise that had an impact on the positive outcome. The scientists and researchers identified these features so they could retest the system using the same protocol as the successful launch.

How many times do we take our successes and failures at face value, without thinking much about them? Likewise, how often do we analyze our failures to identify mistakes (highly recommended) but take our gains for granted? That leads to magical thinking: "I'll never be able to run a mile in less than four minutes again—that was a miracle!" Sure, there's a certain mystery in every conquest, but there are many more specific identifiable elements involved than there is magic.

Success inertia can be stemmed by breaking down our gains and looking at the parts that went into the whole. That's not the same as making the same product long past its market expiration date—it's looking at the parts that went into the success and using them for success in other areas.

Don't Be an Incumbent

Did you ever work in an office where some people seemed stuck in their ways, hesitant to change procedures or diverge from company tradition? I have, too, and we're not imagining it. Employees familiar with processes specific to an organization ("incumbents") often miss opportunities outside their core businesses (think Firestone and Laura Ashley), according to management researchers. As long as they're maintaining a satisfactory level of work, they're not terribly motivated to work harder to innovate.

Turns out that people new to a process, problem, or organization ("entrants") are responsible for the most revolutionary and profitable innovation, according to F. M. Scherer, Professor Emeritus of Public Policy and Corporate Management in the Aetna Chair at Harvard University. Newbies see the possibilities because they're not tied to company convention, history, or the opinions of those who carry the torch of past successes (that's why new people with new ideas often come up against resentment and suspicion from colleagues). They also don't have the luxury or comfort of having had a previous success— so they have to make an effort to earn rave reviews.

So how do you make yourself into a "new" employee in a company you've been with for years? What about asking your boss if you can work in another department? If you have solved problems and discovered new opportunities in your current job, it makes sense to bring those skills to another area and "shake things up." My friend Bob, for example, might have benefited from moving to another area of cell research. If your company is resistant to that idea (they shouldn't be, in my opinion), consider changing firms so you can become an "entrant" again.

If you're a manager at a company, move your employees around so they become "new" employees in a different department or team. Can you devise a new organizational structure in which individual responsibilities and goals change? Change forces employees to innovate and solve problems efficiently. Joining a team of new people also gets employees out of a behavior ditch. Separating employees who have become close friends compels them to exercise their social skills—and it introduces them to new ways of thinking. All of this sparks their creativity.

If you work for yourself, are studying for a degree, or are

pursuing a personal goal outside of the structure of an office or school, there are a few things you can do to "change the scenery." How do you approach your current challenge or project with fresh eyes? First, change the scenery, literally—move where you normally do your work (that's what laptops are for). Sometimes just sitting at a different desk gives you a new outlook or eliminates the usual distractions. Trying to improve a sports technique? Go to another gym or track and work alongside a new set of people. This always gets my adrenaline going—it's the nervous energy of being in a new environment. Switch gears completely—stop working on the project that's giving you difficulty and work on something else on your to-do list. The solution you're looking for often materializes when you've stopped "forcing" yourself to be creative.

Management experts say inertia often happens because we don't have enough—or the right kind of—information to pursue new solutions or actions. Okay, maybe it's time to go back to the drawing board. Just because you've had a breakthrough doesn't mean there's nothing more to learn. Research, read, and study—immerse yourself in your topic. Go to a conference related to your industry (more often than not I find them to be worth the price of admission) and attend networking events and seminars. Find out what's going on in your industry and get your juices flowing.

Look for What's Not Being Done

Careful observers of the "scene" (whatever your scene is) are often able to spot trends and exploit them based on what people *aren't* doing, or based on what they could be doing better. Sometimes looking to the past is a source of great ideas that can be revamped and updated for modern times.

According to my fashion-forward friends, this happens all the time in the clothing business. I recently noticed this phenomenon when I was walking downtown in a large city where I was speaking. One-piece "shorts" jumpsuits, called play suits (I call 'em flight suits, but what do I know?) seemed to be in every other boutique window. Apparently, fashion designers are always scouring not only street fashion but also old pattern catalogs and back issues of fashion magazines to come up with a style that young fashion buyers don't know anything about and the rest of us have conveniently forgotten. All of a sudden one-piece shorts outfits look totally new and now.

A similar phenomenon happened with the PT Cruiser, Chrysler's retro-inspired car that launched in late 1999, with a 2000 model. As soon as the cars rolled off the assembly line consumers were literally lining up to buy this completely new-looking but nostalgic car. Chrysler designer Bryan Nesbitt wanted to evoke an old gangster getaway car or hot rod Model A wagon—sensing that there was a hunger for quirky vintage in the marketplace. After all, this car didn't look anything like the low, modern sedans or boxy SUVs that were being turned out at the time. The car was such a hit that not only were there waiting lists, some people paid more than sticker price just so they could be first on their block to have a PT Cruiser. For a long time it was the best-selling Chrysler-brand vehicle.

After several years, sales started to dip, so in July 2009, PT Cruiser stopped production. I don't think this is a failure—the move to stop production, in fact, is the opposite of success inertia. Would that Firestone had been that savvy. The carmaker could have spent a few more years pushing out PT Cruisers and dealing with the continuous decline of sales. But they didn't—they seemed to sense that the time was right to cut production before they had to cut big losses. This gave them the time and money to look for and design the next big thing. Which leads me to . . .

Stay Connected to the Present

Inertia can strike when we become too consumed with what happened yesterday and what might happen tomorrow. Yes, we need to learn from our failures and successes. And yes, history offers a wealth of inspiration. Once we understand the past's lessons, we have to move on and either avoid making the same mistake twice or implement those actions that were helpful. As for the future, it's important to plan—and we'll do that later in this chapter—but it's a bad idea to "what if" yourself into oblivion.

Bottom line: Be aware of what's come before, and remember the past so you aren't doomed to repeat its failures. Know that tomorrow's possibilities are endless through actions that have an eye on the future, but don't be pulled off course by memories and fantasies. Stay connected. If you're living on past successes, you won't be able to see when they have stopped working. Like I said earlier, by the time you shake yourself out of your stupor, there will be a lot of ground to cover just to get back up to speed.

A buddy of mine wears one of those rubber bracelets on his wrist, and whenever he catches himself thinking too much about Iraq or wondering if his new business is going to take off, he snaps it as a literal reminder to snap out of it and get back to the present. If you don't want to do that, when you catch yourself spending too much time thinking about things that are already dead and buried or events you can't predict, shake your head or do something physical to bring yourself back in the moment. You know that you can't take action anywhere but the here and now.

COMPETITIVE ADVANTAGE

Another way to build on your successes is to understand your competitive advantages and exploit them. In the beginning of the Zero to Breakthrough process, you took note of your skills and unearthed your passions. Identifying your competitive advantages is another step in that process. Now that you have a few breakthroughs under your belt, start looking at the things that make you different as assets, because, well, they are. I'm talking about diversity, not representational diversity, which is usually what diversity officers at companies and institutions mean when they use the word. In this way they are adding people to a group based on what they look like, what color they are, or what ethnic group they belong to, as if this alone will achieve balance and creativity in the workplace. It doesn't.

Believe me, I know about status quo diversity policies. As Diversity Officer for Headquarters Marine Corps and liaison to the Pentagon, I helped a 200,000 personnel organization get back on track. I talk to many organizations each year about diversity in the workforce, and I tell them the same thing I did when I was working on diversity for the Corps. It's not about having X number of whites to X number of blacks to X number of Latinos in an office. When we first start to talk about this, they're skeptical. There's a tendency for human resources managers to just want me to help them hire a few people who don't look like the ones they already have so they can move on to the next assignment. It's just not that easy. And it's certainly not a way to create a winning team.

Think about it this way. Pick any three ethnicities and put three representatives of each in the same room. Now you have nine people in the room and a nice little rainbow of faces. What if it turns out that they all have the same political beliefs, the same work experience, all come from the accounting department, and all have the same strengths and weaknesses? You could end up with nine registered Democrat accountants. Sure, they can produce some good-looking financials; they just can't write a yearly report or create strategic plans. There are no operations people on board. Besides, they're so in sync that they all would agree that the growth strategy the guy in the corner thought up is just dandy. This is not how the most innovative, curious, and energetic teams operate. Okay, this is an exaggeration, but I've been asked to look at team situations that came pretty close.

Combat Confidence: Sameness is static; differences are kinetic. Create more breakthroughs by seeking out unique situations and avoiding the all-too-familiar.

What are the "differences" that a particular company, organization, or group of consumers lacks? In my case, being a black woman definitely would be two advantages for some businesses. Of course, they are not much of an advantage in a business run by black women, but they could be in one run by white guys. It's up to you to sell people on your differences *as advantages to them.* My experiences as female and black are going to give an office of white guys a much-needed perspective (and vice versa—a white guy coming into a black female–owned business might be just the thing the ladies need to bust them out of a rut). Likewise, my experience as an aviator and military officer are differences that could be assets to a group of at-risk teenage girls, no matter what color they are.

Then there's my work style: quick, energetic, creative, and collaborative. That could be just the ticket for a team with too many methodical, analytic, introspective, lone-wolf types. I would add some tension to the group, not because I'm a woman or black, but because my style is different from that of the other employees. The team may not like it at first, but by challenging the group's thinking in ways they've never been challenged before, and in being challenged by them, we'll have more breakthrough ideas. That's genuine diversity—making sure you can bring your talents, skills, experiences, points of view, style, energy, and passions to a place where they will be complemented *and* challenged.

The tension, energy, and chemistry authentic multiplicity creates makes for a powerful breakthrough elixir. Know what you bring to the table so you can make sure you're sitting with the right crowd. Surrounding yourself with yes men or people who think as you do is not going to stretch your successes.

FUTURE PLANNING

More planning? You'd better believe it. Those plans you made back in Chapter 2, need to be revised with an eye on what you've done, what you've learned, and where you're going. I call this future planning—in order to keep flying, you need fuel, and the farther away you get from your starting point, the more necessary it is to have new maps. I was known for carrying a lot of maps with me when I was on a Cobra mission. I had road maps of small areas, maps that covered huge areas of land, and everything in between. From any point I not only needed to know exactly where I was but where I was going.

Future planning is a way of identifying the next goal, revising old goals, and preparing for them *while you're in flight.* Planning by nature is future-oriented, and since the future is uncertain, all planning is based on imperfect knowledge and involves assumptions. By now, however, one thing you have in your favor is experience. You've done some planning, and you've had some breakthroughs. While future planning can never eliminate uncertainty, it does allow you to act effectively and efficiently in the face of uncertainty based on what you know to be true. Besides, having a future plan in place gives you somewhere to go if all else fails.

There's a guy I know, Jack, who left a career in publishing to buy a computer training company. He had done the research on the business in general but hadn't thought that the company's location, in southern Florida, would have any impact on its business cycle. Jack was wrong: It turns out that no one wants to take computer classes in the summer in Florida. By mid-June, sales projections for the season were already off by 50 percent. His solution was to tweak his fall plans so he could launch a set of computer classes that would be of interest to the year-round residents rather than the snowbirds, seasonal families, and single people who gave him a lot of business the rest of the year. Without that plan for the future, Jack would have had to scramble to come up with something to cut his seasonal losses.

Marine commanders use something called critical information requirements, or CCIRs, to identify friendly activities, enemy (competitor) activities, the current environment, and predicted changes to the environment so they can make the most effective future battle plans. For instance, knowing the seasonal changes (environment) to a customer base makes future planning more effective and accurate. Commanders consider CCIRs critical to planning future activities like decision making and situation awareness. CCIRs can be used for your own future planning. And I must say, it's a cool way to do it.

Determine the Facts

Facts are conditions and situations that exist in reality and can be proved with empirical evidence. We all know that. When you are building on successes, it's essential to understand the facts of your situation—from what you've accomplished and learned to date, to who you've met, your financial situation, and anything else that is pertinent to your current state.

Establish assumptions. Assumptions are theories that you believe to be true about your current situation and related future events and conditions. When there's an absence of facts, you have no choice—you have to trust your assumptions, so they had better be good. The following questions will help you determine whether an assumption is valid or off base (answering "no" to one or more signals you may be looking in the wrong direction):

1. Is your assumption logical?
2. Is it based on similar or past experiences?
3. Is it realistic?
4. Is it essential for your plan to work?

> **Combat Confidence:** Flight into the future requires a trio of actions: aviate, navigate, communicate. Aviate means keep flying; navigate means read the map and find your way; communicate means stay in touch as you go—talk to your wingmen and Breakthrough Buddies.

There's a woman, Jean, who runs a tutoring service for high school kids in my town. She has a very good business, as parents want their children to do well in school and increase their chances of getting into a great college. A couple of competitors recently opened up similar businesses, and while Jean is very well known, she realizes that it's not enough to have a great reputation to keep and attract the best customers. The facts: She tutored fifteen students at any one time. As three to four of them left to take finals and graduate, the same number would enter as new clients.

Her assumptions were that she would always have clients as long as she maintained her reputation but that her competitors surely would try to undercut her prices. She made this assumption because she did the same thing when she started in the business. After surveying the competition, she established a price system that was 10 percent below the lowest-priced tutor. As her client base and reputation grew, she charged more.

The fact was that Jean couldn't reduce her prices at this point. She also assumed she would have to enhance her service in some way that would continue to attract the best clients.

Set the Future Game Plan

With the facts and assumptions in front of you, your next step is a battle plan (I like to call it a flight plan). These six questions will help make your plan very clear:

1. *What?* What's your course of action? In Jean's case, she wanted to make two changes to her business. The first was to offer "intensive" sessions that lasted forty-five minutes instead of the usual ninety. She planned to charge less for these sessions, as a way of making her tutoring more accessible without actually reducing her prices. Second, she planned to add college-application and essay counseling to her menu of services.

2. *Why?* It's important to clarify why your plan is necessary to build on your success. Jean wanted to keep her business innovative and responsive to market conditions.

3. *Who?* Is your plan something you can implement on your own? Can you delegate part of it to others? Jean employed two other tutors, and she assigned them the task of developing the intensive sessions while she focused on developing the college application segment of the business.

4. *When?* How soon can you implement the plan—tomorrow, in a month, next year? In Jean's case her plan was to introduce the intensive sessions during the summer, for kids who wanted to stay on top of their studies but also wanted to enjoy the season, take on a summer job, or go to camp. The college application business would be introduced at the beginning of the school year and offered to juniors and seniors. This would give Jean the summer to create the business, schedule advertising, and send mailers to local schools and parents' groups.

5. *Where?* Does your plan require more space or travel, or a change of location? Jean didn't need to move, but she would need to set up another work space for her college application clients.

6. *How?* What are the steps you need to take to implement your plan? How are you going to accomplish it? Jean had to take a series of steps: make sure her tutors designed high-quality intensive tutoring sessions; study the college application process; network with tutors in other cities and states to learn the dos and don'ts to help her develop a successful program; and build an extra work space in her office.

> **Combat Confidence:** You've arrived—in control and making the decision about where you are flying. Think outside the cockpit when you are in the bubble that you have created and stay aware of what's outside that bubble. Know where the enemy is hiding, keep contact with friendly troops, and identify and follow the clear paths.

BREAK POINT CASE STUDY: ECLECTIC SUCCESS

I log a lot of airplane passenger hours, so I end up reading many local newspapers and magazines. On one flight I read an amazing interview with Dave Austin, a former world-ranked pro tennis player, Hollywood actor, singer, record producer, and real estate developer, who several years ago founded a company that provides "mental performance coaching" for professional athletes, corporate executives, and anyone who wants to exceed their potential. That last part got me pretty interested in this guy—Austin is the perfect example of someone who understands his competitive advantages and has managed to exploit them in a unique way.

The story was about Austin's idea for a weekly Internet television series, called *Beyond the Field: Players of Faith*, which features top athletes' insights into what motivates them to succeed in their sport. "Internet television is growing, so I thought, 'Why not take people behind the scenes with me to

really find what makes these players tick beyond their sport,'"
he told the reporter.

Cool, but what particularly got my attention was Austin's
description of his work as a mental performance coach. "My
work is really about the process. It's not about the results." He
says that the results take care of themselves once you learn to
appreciate and love the process. Austin was born in Oakland;
his dad was Henry Austin, who was a U.S. Navy chaplain.
When he discovered a love of and a talent for sports and athlet-
ics, he went out for whatever sports were offered at his school.

When coaches told him he was good, he would be really
good. "In football I'd run for touchdown after touchdown,"
he says. But when an angry coach in North Carolina told him
he was terrible, he fulfilled his words by being really lousy. "I
became what he told me I was." Luckily, when the family moved
to Hawaii, Austin had a supportive coach. All of a sudden he
was running fast again. It didn't take long for him to figure out
that if you believe in yourself and your abilities and reject the
unnecessary put-downs of others, you become what you are.

From that discovery, Austin built one athletic success on
another. He surfed in world championships, went to college on
football and baseball scholarships, won a tennis scholarship to
San Diego State University, and in the late 1970s went on the
World Tennis Tour for a year.

Austin played the tennis tournament circuit for five years.
While competing in the Carl Reiner Celebrity Tournament in
La Costa, a casting director spotted him and asked if he would
be interested in reading for a movie. "When you allow yourself
to be fully present and you're passionate about something, I have

the belief you can do anything," he says. Austin said yes, went to audition, got the part, and moved to Los Angeles—just like that.

That was thirty-seven years ago, and Austin says he still earns residuals from his first movie. He's worked with Gene Hackman on *Uncommon Valor*, and *Jagged Edge* with Glenn Close and Jeff Bridges, as well as a television series, *The Oldest Rookie*, and a miniseries, *Robert F. Kennedy and His Times*, along with a host of television commercials for Diet Coke, Burger King, Chevron, Molson Beer, and Olympia Beer.

Meanwhile, he built on his work as an actor to pursue another dream—singing. He joined his friend Phil Earhart, who founded the rock band Kansas, and did what he says was the first celebrity charity concert. He also sang in concerts with Queen, Santana, Kansas, REO Speedwagon, and other bands. In 1991, he even won a Grammy—the Presidential Merit Award for his work raising money for charities through concerts. It doesn't stop there—Austin formed the record label Granite Records, and in 1999, he wrote and published a faith-based book, *Listen to the Voice Within*.

He discovered that his experiences as a competitive athlete and performer seemed to mirror the epiphany he had when he was a young man—believing in yourself allows you to exceed expectations. He felt that was something he could share with athletes, performers, and businesspeople. The way Austin explains it, mental performance coaching is different from sports psychology.

Since he was a professional athlete and a businessperson, he learned firsthand what works and what doesn't work for you when you're competing. "If I'm going to get stronger physically, I'm going to lift weights. But if I'm going to get stronger mentally, I need to know processes that can help my mind work for me rather than against me," he explained. In addition to working with professional athletes, he coaches corporate executives because the same principles apply—the competitors are there, too; they're just wearing a suit and tie instead of a uniform.

When he began working with the U.S. Olympic field hockey team and the Los Angeles Dodgers as a mental performance coach, he met a literary agent who had read and loved the book. He approached him to write a very different book, *Songwriting for Dummies*, which he worked on with his wife and songwriter Jim Peterik ("Eye of the Tiger" fame), and which went on to become a bestseller.

Austin found his passion and turned it into a lucrative career by being self-aware, never saying no, and applying what he learned in each job to the next one. Let's look at what Austin did:

1. **Had self-awareness:** Austin's self-knowledge led to a brilliant insight that eventually became the basis for his career—positive reinforcement leads to success, while put-downs lead to failure. You can give yourself that positive reinforcement if you know how to.

2. **Avoided success inertia:** Be open to new ways of doing things and change up your routine whenever possible. Austin didn't coast on his tennis chops—otherwise he might have wound up an aging tennis pro at a run-down resort. He used his athleticism to become an actor and his acting skills to become a speaker and communicator. He never let success in one area stand in his way.

3. **Never said no to an opportunity:** Find ways to transfer your skills in one area to another (sportsman to speaker and coach, television actor to Internet television producer).

4. **Exploited his competitive advantages:** Austin has been an athlete, actor, and writer. He uses all of those skills as a mental performance coach. He understands the competitor's mind (whether athlete or businessperson); he knows how to communicate and project on screen, in person, and on paper. Everything he has done in his life has been a building block for his current business.

BREAK POINT CASE STUDY: BLOCKBUSTED!

I love movies, but I can't remember the last time I visited a "video" store, can you? The home-movie business sure has changed—technology has made it possible for you and me to sit down, turn on the flat screen, and order up any movie we want. The technology continues to grow, and how and where we can watch movies is constantly evolving. Back in the mid-1980s and early 1990s there was a mom-and-pop movie rental shop on every other block in urban areas and at least two or three in small towns. Movie rental stores had gone from sleazy places in the worst parts of town to mainstream outlets for wholesome family entertainment. Many were small businesses run by single owners serving their local community, but some entrepreneurs had a larger vision for the at-home movie market.

David Cook was one such businessman. He had made money writing computer programs for the oil business and other industries and was looking for another industry to invest in. In 1985, Cook's wife, Sandy, saw a growing niche market for video rentals. She was an avid movie fan and figured if small stores were doing well renting out movies to locals, a large store with a huge variety of flicks to choose from—recently released titles, genre films, classics, documentaries, and kids' stuff—would draw even more customers.

The Blockbuster story itself could be a movie; it is filled with a huge cast of characters, ups and downs, obvious missteps, and emotion. The Cooks opened their first store in 1985, and a year later Cook gave the store a new name—Blockbuster Entertainment. Cook funded the first store by selling off his existing oil and gas software business. He wanted the store to have the best-stocked shelves in town, so that first store carried eight thousand individual tapes, an unprecedented number at the time. Don't they say that everything in Texas is big? I guess he was living up to that.

Back then tapes were relatively expensive to buy, averaging about $70 per movie, so his inventory costs alone were about $560,000. His instinct to put down that kind of investment was right, as the store was a huge success and each movie made its money back within months. By 1986, Cook had opened three more Blockbuster Entertainment stores. Blockbuster's motto and mission was to turn ordinary family nights into "blockbuster nights."

The next twenty years were a roller-coaster ride for Blockbuster; it weathered a few financial storms, but the company grew into a world-class operation with thousands of locations and billions of dollars in revenue. Here are a few of the highlights (I'm telling you, this is truly an epic business story). By September 1986, Cook needed to raise capital for expansion, which led to an initial public offering, or IPO. However, on the day before the offering, a damaging news article about Cook's computer business delayed the stock offering. This resulted in liquidity problems for the company, and they ended the year with a $3.2 million loss.

In early 1987, Cook sold a one-third stake in the company to a group of investors lead by Wayne Huizenga. In exchange, Blockbuster got an infusion of $18.6 million—but Cook was forced to turn over future control of the company, and he left the company altogether by April. With Huizenga in control, Blockbuster began a rapid expansion program. Huizenga bought up rival chains to expand his customer base. In 1993, media giant Viacom merged with Blockbuster, but the marriage was rocky and investors were not too pleased, so stocks in both companies dropped. Huizenga split.

The new managers who came in had a negative influence on company performance, but they didn't stay long. In 1997, John Antioco took over as chairperson and CEO. He was able to get Blockbuster on even footing in part by forcing movie studios to change the way they were paid, which reduced Blockbuster's costs significantly. The company continued to grow in terms of store size, but it didn't always post profits; it often posted losses. In 2004, Viacom spun the company off, and the chain tried to prove it could survive and thrive as an independent company.

Fast-forward six years. Between 2007 and 2010, the company

lost more than $1 billion as a result of store closings, declining sales, and consumers who found other ways to access movies more conveniently. As of July 2010, Blockbuster had become a money-losing enterprise struggling to find itself in a world now dominated by on-demand movies, downloadable movies, Netflix, and other technological advances that the company has never seemed to be able to exploit. Bondholders had to agree to let the company defer a $42.4 million payment on its 11.75 percent notes for a month as it tried to find recapitalization. Trading in Blockbuster stock shares was halted in 2010, and the company was delisted from the New York Stock Exchange.

I'm not a professor of management, so I can't give you heavy technical theories on why Blockbuster has failed and is now more or less on life support. But just reading this summary of the company's story shows how tempting it is to accelerate too quickly. Let's look at some of Blockbuster's missteps:

1. **Did too much too fast:** The company was successful from the start but in a short amount of time was looking for capital to expand. This isn't necessarily a bad strategy, but it might have been better to expand with company profits than to look for investors who take your rights, passion, and vision away in exchange for cash.

2. **Suffered from success inertia:** This syndrome led Blockbuster to make deals with big movie companies as a strategy for growth instead of looking for ways to stay on top of innovative technology. In the end, that's what really sealed their fate—renting DVDs from

a store? So forever ago—and such a pain in the you-know-what. That's hard to overcome.

3. **Ignored its competitive advantage:** What about those powerful relationships with movie studios, a large electronic database of customers along with their rental habits, and an inventory of millions of individual titles? Blockbuster could have been Netflix before Netflix came along; they could have invested in technology to bring Blockbuster right to movie buffs' screens, whether it was on a television, computer, or cell phone. But they didn't see their advantages in that context, or if they did, they couldn't exploit them fast enough.

4. **Had limited future planning:** Finally, Blockbuster's future planning seems limited to constantly looking for ways to find cash. It's tough to do much else if you can't pay your bills.

Z2B EXERCISE: TAKE YOUR SUCCESS TEMPERATURE

Once you've had some breakthroughs, it's helpful to make a list of them, how you accomplished them, and, perhaps most important, how you feel about them. They don't have to be major breakthroughs—we can have small breakthroughs that build up into major breakthroughs. Writing down what you've accomplished in a log does a few things. First, anytime you put something in writing, it becomes real—it's official.

Second, when you keep track of those small steps forward, it becomes a visual of your progress. It's like watching your personal stock go up, up, up—very motivating. Finally, taking time to review what you've done can become an exercise in gratitude, and I think that is so important. Every time you have a little victory, make a discovery, or meet someone who can help you—acknowledge it and say thank you. Gratitude puts you in a very motivated state of mind.

Z2B EXERCISE: IDENTIFY YOUR STRATEGIC ADVANTAGES

What are yours? Evaluating them is not as easy as it sounds, as they can include everything from where you grew up to what you look like to what you know. Any given aspect of your personality or life could be an asset to someone or to yourself as you pursue your passion. A wingman or BTB can help out in this exercise, as he or she may see advantages that you take for granted. I was talking to a friend of mine about being a Marine recruit. She had read an article about the Crucible and asked me if I had to go into the Gas Chamber. "Of course I did, every recruit has to do it," I said. She asked me why I had never mentioned it, and I told her I just thought everyone knew about that. "Uh-uh, Vernice," she said, "Marines might know about it, but I'm pretty sure the average civilian walking around isn't aware of that."

She reminded me that this unique experience gave me a strategic advantage over someone who hadn't gone through it. How so? Well, I have demonstrated that I can stay calm and focused during a crisis, I do not lose my cool, and I am not adversely impacted by chaos around me. That gives me a strategic advantage in any kind of high-stress job. If I wanted to, I probably could convince someone to give me a job on the floor of the New York Stock Exchange—even though I'm not a financial whiz, I have some of the basic qualities necessary to be good at trading. If you have the important qualities for a specific activity or job, the rest is just details—which you can learn.

Once you're done with the list, take time over a few days to study it—how can these advantages help you pursue your passion and meet your goals?

Z2B EXERCISE: CREATE A FUTURE PLAN

Using the Future Planning section on the next two pages as a guide, map out what your next steps will be. Copy and use this form if you like, or download it from my Web site, www.vernicearmour.com.

FUTURE PLANNING WORKSHEET

Facts of My Situation _____

_____

_____

_____

_____

_____

Assumptions About Present and Future Conditions _____

_____

_____

_____

_____

1. Are my assumptions logical? _____

_____

_____

_____

2. Are they realistic? _____

_____

_____

_____

3. Are they essential for my plan to work? _____

_____

_____

_____

_____

MY FLIGHT PLAN

Mission: _____

_____

_____

_____

1. What? _____

_____

_____

_____

2. Why? _____

_____

_____

_____

3. Who? _____

_____

_____

_____

4. When? _____

_____

_____

_____

5. Where? _____

_____

_____

_____

6. How? _____

_____

_____

_____

OPERATION FUTURE FREEDOM

In February 2004, the Commandant of the Marine Corps, Michael W. Hagee, gave the Senate Armed Services Committee a statement on the Marine Corps's "posture," or state of readiness, especially concerning preparation for Operation Iraqi Freedom II. In this report, he talked about analyzing lessons learned from, among other experiences, conducting security and stability operations in Iraq from March to September 2003. He described how Marine Expeditionary Forces worked closely with the Army forces in Iraq using military procedures and even law enforcement strategies such as those used by the Los Angeles Police Department to patrol, control, and break up gang-controlled neighborhoods.

"We have assimilated these lessons through a comprehensive training package that includes tactics, techniques, procedures for stability, and counter-insurgency operations," he wrote, "... paying particular attention to individual protective equipment [and] enhanced vehicle and aircraft hardening, and aviation survival training and support are critically important as we send Marines back to war in a volatile, dangerous, and changing situation." Military talk, for sure. But what Hagee is really saying is that even though the Marines, and the U.S. military for that matter, are a highly trained, elite group of men and women, there's always something new to understand about their jobs as both warriors and peacekeepers.

That's pretty much how I see Flight and Future—a revolving and evolving series of lessons to be learned, techniques to enhance, strategies to improve upon. The more you know, the more comfortable you are about shifting and modifying strategies, and the freer you are to pursue your passions. It's this process that makes Zero to Breakthrough so exciting—if you respect the process, the results take care of themselves. There is never a point where you stop training; there's always more to learn. You can make the decision to stop or change course, but that doesn't mean there isn't more for you out there if you decide to get back in the helicopter and take off from wherever you are.

FLY-AWAYS

- Don't be a victim of success inertia.

- Stay in the present, be mindful of the past, and keep an eye on the future.

- Identify and exploit your competitive advantages.

- Plan for the future using the facts and best assumptions.

CHAPTER 7

Any Given Dream:
The Breakthrough Moment

*Rejoice at your achievements; you are honoring
the legacy that got you there.*

—VERNICE "FLYGIRL" ARMOUR

Remember the tactics test I took and failed? I felt as if I had diminished a standard I needed—and wanted—to uphold. The next week, I took the test again and passed with flying colors, but in my mind the damage had been done. I wasn't even close to being put on the fast track. I spent another two and a half years in the squadron, which included another tour in Iraq.

At the end of that stint, the Corps transferred me to the East Coast, to Quantico, Virginia, to fulfill my headquarters tour. Things were less intense, certainly, and I did my job effectively and with good cheer. Except that even years later I could not get that failed tactics test out of my mind; it hung over my head like a dark cloud. Was there any significance to that failure? As I would soon find out, every decision we make has repercussions beyond the obvious.

It was around ten o'clock one night, and I was having a heart-to-heart with a close friend in her car, after a meeting. I was discussing things I'd never shared with anyone else before; outside of the car it would have felt like I was whining. It felt good to unpack some of these old feelings. Had I passed and done well on the tactics test the first time around, I would have been put on the fast track and maybe even sent to WTI (Weapons and Tactics Instructor course), the Marines' version of Top Gun. I would have wound up back in Iraq again, but in a different role with new responsibilities. As I listened to myself, it dawned on me that, had I passed the test the first time, I wouldn't have met the people or had the experiences I'd had in the previous year. I wouldn't have gone to the Women of Color in Technology conference, where the seed was planted to become a professional speaker, my true passion. But most important, I wouldn't have been sitting at a desk to answer the phone when my mom called on a Wednesday afternoon.

I could always tell when she was feeling down. She told me Dad was in the hospital. After three tours in Vietnam, some of the chemicals he was exposed to finally had taken their toll. Several years before, he'd been diagnosed with prostate cancer. It had now metastasized into terminal bone cancer, and he was fighting for his life. His blood count was low and he was in the hospital for more blood work. It was looking as though he was going to be in the hospital until Saturday, my mom's birthday. After we hung up, I quickly bought a ticket home.

She was overjoyed when I walked through the door Saturday morning. I wiped her tears. Around 2 p.m., we headed up to see Dad. He was surprised, and happy to see me.

"Hey, baby! How're you doing? I didn't know you were coming home this weekend!"

It was great to see him. He was my favorite Marine.

By 6:07 p.m., Dad had passed away. In just those few hours, he was gone. While I would miss him, his death was somewhat of a relief because he had been in constant pain. He was a fighter to the end. But now he seemed at peace, and I was blessed to have been by his side.

All my experiences—including that tactics test—had led me to being with him in that moment. My dad is gone. But what he stood for, his legacy, is continuing in and through me. What I've come to realize is that everything that happens in life helps to shape our legacies. I had a choice to study for the first test, but I made a different choice. I chose to do better the next time and accepted the consequences of my actions. You have to own what you do, and see every outcome as perfect. Aside from that, I realized that how you react to disappointments and victories contributes to your legacy and determines what kind of leader you'll be. Many times we question why we have certain experiences. Les Brown has a great quote: "You can't see the picture when you're in the frame." I wouldn't change a thing about failing that tactics test—it took me years to realize that.

When I saw that black woman in a flight suit years ago, a very powerful seed was planted. It was a seed so strong that, years after it was planted, it sprouted with life. This wasn't TV, this was my reality! I not only saw the possibility, I could actually touch her. She was tangible. I refer to the moment of seeing her as the "tangibility of the possibility." It changed my life. I am also *her* legacy.

Becoming a *tangibility of the possibility* for other women was one of my ultimate breakthroughs. The impact I could have on other people—women, kids, black people, anyone really, who had an "impossible dream"—was made very clear to me when I appeared on *The Oprah Winfrey Show* (twice!). Reaching a lot of people at once with my message certainly was one way of having an impact.

The first time I was "on" the show, I was actually in Kuwait during the Iraq invasion. The public affairs person on base told me Oprah wanted to interview me on her show via telephone. My parents would be in the studio. I had always known I would be on *Oprah* someday—was this it? While I told Oprah this, she said something like, "Oh, I know, your mom tells me you love the Omni Hotel we mention at the end of each show." The audience cracked up, and I said, "Yes I always wanted to be on, but I never pictured it would be like this—my parents in the audience and staying at the Omni, and me on the phone from Kuwait."

Oprah promised me, on the air, that when I got back from Iraq she would have me on the show in person. Flash-forward several months: I was back at home and walking down a hall at the base when an officer came up to me and said, "The CO [commanding officer] wants to talk to you." Oh, no, I thought, what did I do now? As you might have figured out by now, trouble is my middle name. When I got to the CO's office, he was walking out while I was walking in. I almost jumped out of my boots. "It's okay, Armour, you're wanted on the phone," he said. Huh? Oh, no. What did Mom do now—why is she calling the CO's office?

I picked up the phone, and it wasn't my mother. It was a producer from *Oprah*. She told me that Oprah wanted me. "You'll have four days off—we've cleared it with your CO. Go home and pack and be at the airport tomorrow." I was excited, to say the least—it was one of the moments I had dreamed about, and it had been realized. I had even rehearsed my opening line: "Well, Oprah, it was like this . . ." More important, it was the first time *I* had learned that I was—and was truly recognized for being—the first black female Marine combat pilot in U.S. history. It very possibly could be a breakthrough for all the folks watching who were striving for something that seemed out of reach.

Do you know now that you can accomplish any mission you give yourself? Breakthrough goes beyond one accomplishment; it's bigger than reaching a destination and continuing the flight. We are standing on many shoulders, and we must continue to lay the foundation and take positive steps while teaching by word, deed, and example those who are coming up behind us. Our ancestors gave blood, sweat, and tears—they also gave their very lives for us to have the opportunities that exist today. We are standing on their shoulders, and I hope that the generation to come can stand on ours.

Legacy is the power we all have to make a lasting impression in the way we conduct ourselves, interact with others, and, yes, lead. We are making an impact—a bigger one than we imagine. In the 1960s, Dr. Martin Luther King Jr. reached out to actress Nichelle Nichols when he found out that she was considering quitting her ground-breaking role as Lieutenant Uhura on the original *Star Trek*. This space traveler of African-American descent was the first recurring role for a woman on television.

King told Nichols she needed to remain on the show playing that character, for it was also a rare opportunity for people to see a black woman playing something other than a role of servitude. Some years later, Nichols used the celebrity, visibility, and credibility she created through the popular series to recruit and facilitate the selection of the first women and minority astronauts for the NASA Space Shuttle program. Something NASA had been unable to do without her.

What legacy are you leaving? When you showed up, the world was in a certain condition. Will it be a better place when you leave? Is your family a better family with you in it? Are your friends inspired by you? When you leave your job, is that company going to be better off because you were there? What seeds are you planting in others? You don't live or work in a vacuum. Being a leader is more than just doing a great job or managing people well. You've got to step out of that role once in a while in order to be better at it—and in order to establish broad shoulders for others to stand on.

These are some ways to live as a leader and leave a legacy:

1. *Get involved.* Sit on a committee at work, join business associations, become a member of one of your town's committees—something that interests you (like a parks committee, historical society, or local political group). Local committees are always looking for volunteers.

2. *Join a non-profit board.* Non-profit boards are easier to volunteer for or be invited to be a part of than are corporate boards. My friend Karen sat on the board of

a nursing home for several years, and it was one of the most rewarding experiences she'd ever had. She learned a lot about leadership that she could apply to her private-sector job, and she felt she made a real difference to how the home was run and the quality of life of the residents.

3. *Volunteer.* Join Habitat for Humanity, work at a soup kitchen, help out at a hospital (when I was a teenager, they called them candy stripers) or an animal shelter. Breaking out of your normal routine and being conscious of how other people live is enriching and, frankly, offers the benefits of empathy, sympathy, and understanding to your role as a businessperson, manager, and leader.

4. *Start a foundation.* Unlike establishing a charity, creating a foundation is relatively easy and is a wonderful way to help other individuals, organizations, and causes through grant money.

5. *Help your candidate.* Depending on your skills, volunteer as a door-knocker, writer, office helper, or fundraiser.

6. *Be a good citizen and a great neighbor.* This one's easy—we all should be building our legacy this way.

WAKE UP A LEADER

As I said in the very beginning of this book, the Marine Corps believes that leaders are made, not born. And to prove it they turn out thousands of leaders each year. We're trained to put ourselves directly into harm's way and risk our own lives to accomplish a mission. Fred Smith, the founder of FedEx, paid tribute to the vital role the Marine Corps played in his life and success in a 2001 article he wrote for the newsletter

Legacy: "Nothing has prepared business leaders better for their roles in business and society than the lessons they learned in the Corps—lessons of discipline, organization, commitment, and integrity." That is the common goal of the Corps and Zero to Breakthrough: to help you become a leader.

Great achievements are wonderful personal milestones. The real point of breakthrough is to better the lives of the people around you. So many people focus on the money end of success and leadership. While I've got nothing against making money, it's not the single thing that you should pursue at any price. Being a leader and doing what you love naturally leads to prosperity. Become a leader and a role model for those around you and for those who will come after you, and to honor those whose shoulders you stand on.

No breakthrough is possible without the people who came before you and broke the ground you now walk on. One of the most important breakthroughs you can have is to inspire someone else rise out of their condition and make it better. You actually can become a leader right now, today—even if you've only started having breakthroughs. *By acting like a leader, you will be a leader.* The great thing about being a leader is that you don't need a company to run, you don't need a lot of money, and you don't need an Ivy League education. We tend to think of these elements as part and parcel of great leaders, but they really aren't. Simply by exemplifying the qualities of a leader, you become one. You're ready.

FOURTEEN TRAITS OF A TRUE LEADER

There are fourteen leadership traits that all Marines have to memorize and demonstrate. When I learned about them, it struck me that there is nothing about these fourteen qualities that is necessarily exclusive to the Marines—they didn't invent them; they just made them official. Everyone can benefit from practicing these traits and finding ways to incorporate them into their own lives and business practices. If you've been reading the book straight through, you'll notice that these are traits I've talked about in one form or another from the very beginning. Now it's time to put them all together and start living them.

> **Combat Confidence:** Stand tall and work your presence: Believe in yourself, and you will find that your leadership qualities emerge. Do what is necessary to generate work that you are proud of and that you can stand behind.

The fourteen traits are:

1. Justice
2. Judgment
3. Dependability
4. Initiative
5. Decisiveness
6. Tact
7. Integrity
8. Enthusiasm
9. Bearing
10. Unselfishness
11. Courage
12. Knowledge

13. Loyalty

14. Endurance

A little trick the Marines use to remember these traits is to use this silly acronym: J.J. DID TIE BUCKLE. Each letter corresponds to the first letter of the traits, in order.

Justice is the practice of being fair and consistent. A just person does not make faulty assumptions about themselves or other people. Just people give consideration to each side of a situation, hear all parties out, and base rewards or punishments on merit. Practice being just by always being honest with yourself, even when it hurts, especially when it comes to why you made a certain decision or took a specific course of action. Don't play favorites—make your best effort to be fair at all times and treat people equally.

Judgment is the ability to think clearly, calmly, and logically so you can make good decisions. Practice good judgment by avoiding making decisions based on emotions like fear, excitement, or sadness. Instead, take a step back and use common sense.

Dependability means that others can count on you to honor your word, follow through with promises, and perform duties and obligations properly and with good cheer. It means that you can be trusted to put your best effort into a job and to complete it as promised. Practice dependability by showing up on time, only promising to do things you actually can do, never breaking a promise or a confidence, and carrying out every responsibility you have to the best of your ability regardless of whether you like it or not.

Initiative is taking action on your own when you see something that needs to be done. It means not waiting around for someone else to tell you what to do. Initiative is also being resourceful, especially when resources are few and far between. Initiative is creative in this sense—you have to use your skills, quick thinking, and enthusiasm. People with initiative tend to be mentally and physically alert.

Decisiveness is the ability to make a good decision and be confident that it was the right one at the right time. It's about gathering as many facts as you can and weighing them calmly and quickly—and listening to your gut. Once you've made up your mind, make your decision known clearly and respectfully but firmly.

Tact is a way of relating to people—with the goodwill, respect, and old-fashioned politeness that your mother and grandmother taught you! It also means showing compassion and empathy for others. You don't know the kind of day a person had or what kind of burdens he or she carries—so keep that in mind during every encounter. When you are courteous and cheerful, others usually will treat you in kind. This makes life a whole lot easier.

Integrity is just a fancy way of saying you should be honest in all of your dealings, personal and professional. Be true to yourself and your values and principles, and respect others by always telling the truth and "doing the right thing." Stand up for what you believe in.

Enthusiasm is a sincere show of optimism and interest in your responsibilities, obligations, and everyday tasks. When you tackle your daily to-do list with zest, the toils of the day seem smaller and the joys so much more pronounced. Changes to your environment and plans are met with much less fear and anxiety if you have a natural enthusiasm and curiosity. Nothing beats enthusiasm!

Bearing is the way you carry yourself. One of the benefits of physical exercise and fitness is that it helps you with your stance and posture. Of course, bearing is more than just standing tall with your shoulders thrown back. It's the vibe you give off— confident, approachable, helpful, and friendly, the kind of person who isn't content just being average or doing only what's required.

Unselfishness means not doing something for yourself at the expense of another person. That means being considerate in the most old-fashioned way (like offering a seat to someone who looks tired or unwell or is pregnant or elderly). It means sharing credit with people who helped you get something done and making sure they are recognized for their contributions. It means never using your position for selfish personal gain. And it means sharing yourself, your experience, and your knowledge with others.

Courage is acknowledging your fear but staying calm and facing it. There is also moral courage, which some people have a harder time with than facing an enemy in hand-to-hand combat. Moral courage is having the strength to stand up for what's right and accepting the blame when you've done something wrong.

Knowledge is being well versed in your subject of choice, but it also means continuously seeking out information, truth, and understanding. There's another aspect to knowledge, and that's "emotional intelligence." You've probably heard this expression before. It's developing insight about others, understanding how to "read" a room or situation accurately. I also think it's very important to be as well-rounded as you can be. That doesn't mean you have to be an expert in everything or, heaven forbid, a know-it-all. It just means your interests should be broad and your curiosity boundless.

Loyalty means showing devotion to your country, your family, job, friends, and so on—whatever and whoever it is that's important in your life. In Chapter 1, I closed with a short section called Always Faithful, as in *semper fidelis*, the motto of the Marines. Loyalty goes a long way in preserving relationships. Being true to yourself and others involves never breaking a confidence or discussing the problems someone has entrusted to you publicly or even privately with another person. If you're in a position to follow orders or take responsibility, carry out orders and responsibilities with the same trust and honor you would expect of others.

Endurance is mental and physical stamina. It's measured by your ability to withstand pain, fatigue, stress, deprivation, and hardship. Enduring pain during a training march is crucial in the development of leaders in the military. It helps in any endeavor—the more you can endure physically and emotionally, the stronger and more compassionate a leader you become. Work your endurance "muscle" by working out, exercising daily, pushing your limits whenever possible, and finishing every task you undertake, including the unpleasant ones.

> The middle of the road is where the white line is, and
> that's the worst place to drive.
>
> —ROBERT FROST, POET

As if fourteen weren't enough, I've compiled five more principles that are common to the best leaders in both military and civilian life. Whenever I get a chance to talk to someone who has made a difference in the world or created a business or organization I admire, I ask them about the one principle that guided them through good times and bad. I never let an opportunity in front of a smart person pass me by. This section represents their most frequent answers. Some of them are extensions of the basic Marine traits, others apply very specifically to those of you who are managing and mentoring others.

Combat Confidence: An idea that has guided me since I was a little girl and always wanted an ever-bigger pony is that I am an individual with free will. The value of independence just cannot be underestimated. As a leader you're obligated to demonstrate and promote the idea that people are responsible for their actions and can achieve breakthroughs, joy, and authentic self-esteem by taking ownership of their lives and never blaming "fate" for their circumstances.

1. *Self-improvement.* No matter how much a person achieves, there always are opportunities for self-expansion and discovery and to gain new insights. There's just no such thing as knowing too much or having too many skills. The leaders I've talked to look at their lives as lives of continual growth.

2. *Accountability.* By taking on more and bigger responsibilities, leaders show that they have confidence in their ability to get the job done and take responsibility if they fall short of expectations. It's easy to take credit when things go well; it takes courage and maturity to be accountable when decisions

or execution of plans don't turn out as planned. Everyone makes mistakes; leaders own up to them.

3. *Trust in others.* Nothing gets done if you can't trust your team. Leaders build teams of people who they trust to get the job done—and they empower them to do their jobs independently. That requires hiring the right people, understanding them, and identifying their strengths and weaknesses so they can be put in positions where they thrive, contribute, and produce the best results. An organization can be stuffed with brainy college graduates, but they won't be successful unless they are placed in positions where they can learn, grow, and succeed.

4. *Steadfastness and consistency.* It is so important to "be there" as a leader. Leaders are predictable in that the people around them know what to expect (no crazy fits or uncontrollable rages when things don't go their way). Leaders demonstrate through word and deed that they're trying their hardest to make decisions that are best for the group and that they are doing the right thing. If a team isn't confident that a leader knows what to do, the trust is broken.

For instance, if I had shouted "guns" into the intercom, I know for a fact that Major Ruvalcaba would have stopped shooting rockets in order to allow me to shoot guns. He trusted that I knew I was making a decision that was best for the mission—and that I had seen a target that needed immediate prosecution. A moment's hesitation in that environment could have meant someone's life.

5. *Communication.* It's impossible to tell each individual on your team or organization what's going on in detail. In the first place, there's simply no time for it—you'd be talking nonstop. However, it is important to have open lines of communication,

to update teams on important developments, and to give people the information they need to do their jobs well.

BREAK POINT CASE STUDY:
LEADERSHIP FROM THE GROUND UP

Ursula M. Burns is a woman I can relate to. She's the chairwoman and CEO of Xerox—the first black woman CEO to head an S&P 100 company. She's also the first woman to succeed another woman as head of an S&P 100 company. I love firsts. In 2009, *Forbes* magazine rated Burns the fourteenth most powerful woman in the United States.

Burns grew up in Baruch Houses, a project located on Delancey Street on the Lower East Side of Manhattan. "There were lots of Jewish immigrants, fewer Hispanics and African-Americans, but the common denominator and great equalizer was poverty," she told a reporter. Her single mom raised her; she was the middle child of three who were born to two different fathers. Neither man participated much in the family's life, and her mother took in ironing and ran a day-care center from home so she could send all her children to Catholic schools. Burns attended Cathedral High School, an all-girls school on East Fifty-sixth Street in Manhattan. "She felt it was the only way to get us good educations and keep us safe," recalled Burns later.

A whiz at math, Burns earned an engineering degree from the Polytechnic Institute of New York. Xerox's graduate engineering program for minorities paid for part of her graduate work at Columbia, and included a summer internship at Xerox.

After Burns graduated with a Master of Science in mechanical engineering, she joined Xerox full-time.

In 1981, Xerox was having some success inertia of its own. They had made the mistake of ignoring the growth in Japanese copiers and new office printers, failing to bring their own innovative products to market. Burns took on roles of increasing responsibility and distinguished herself as a quick study who could solve problems and handle multiple tasks well, and she wasn't afraid to point out problems. In 1990, Wayland Hicks, then a senior executive, offered her a job as his executive assistant. Burns thought it sounded like a dead-end job, but she accepted it.

Nothing could have been further from the truth. What she learned later was that executive assistant jobs at Xerox were not secretarial positions. They were the jobs that division presidents put their best people in. Most of them were white males, so having an African-American female in such a position of power was both a signal of Burns's potential and a signal to other women and minorities in the company that anything was possible at Xerox.

Burns rose through the ranks, becoming executive assistant to then chairman and chief executive Paul Allaire in 1991 and eventually becoming vice president for global manufacturing in 1999. She has overseen several areas of the company, including product development and marketing, engineering, manufacturing, and a number of product divisions.

In 2000, she was named a senior vice president and began working closely with soon to be CEO Anne Mulcahy in what both women describe as a true partnership. In 2002, Burns was named president of Xerox Business Group Operations, businesses that accounted for more than 80 percent of Xerox's sales, as well as the engineering, manufacturing, and other logistical functions that were the backbone of the company's operations.

When she was president of the company, she told an audience at the YWCA in Cleveland, "I'm in this job because I believe I earned it through hard work and high performance. Did I get some opportunities early in my career because of my race and gender? Probably. I went to work for a company that was openly seeking to diversify its workforce. So I imagine race and gender got the hiring guys' attention. And then the rest was really up to me."

Learning about leaders like Burns, who beat the odds, overcame obstacles, and succeeded in historic ways is inspiring and useful to my own efforts to be the best leader I can be. Let's break down a few points about Burns's experience that evoke basic values, common sense, and hard work:

1. **Pursued what she was good at:** Burns was lucky and found what she excelled at early on—math and technology—and pursued it. She was also fortunate to have a mom who believed in education and made sure that Burns and her brothers were exposed to the best possible schools.

2. **Used her competitive advantages:** Burns used her competitive advantages (gender, race, and high math proficiency) to score a great entry-level job at Xerox, one that helped pay for her education. As she says herself, the rest was up to her, and she was determined to prove herself.

3. **Practiced loyalty, trust, and determination:** Which one of the fourteen leadership traits does Burns *not*

exemplify? Her story is one of commitment, account-ability, and hard work. If she could go from a housing project in New York City to the corner office at Xerox, what's your excuse?

BREAK POINT CASE STUDY: ONE DROP OF WATER

It never ceases to amaze how a single person's idea, when acted upon, can create ripples of change that make an enormous dif-ference in other people's lives. Adnan Mahmud, a thirty-one-year-old program manager at Microsoft Research, is a perfect example of how you can be a change maker in the world without the resources or connections of a Bill Gates or Warren Buffett.

Adnan was visiting his grandfather's grave on a trip home to Bangladesh. On his way there he passed a stranger carrying his dead son, who was dressed only in a pair of shorts. The man was so poor he couldn't afford the traditional white cloth used to shroud the dead for a proper Muslim burial.

"There were vendors selling cloth for fifty cents or a dollar," Mahmud said. He easily could have bought a cloth for the man but didn't think of it until he was already back home in Califor-nia. Still, the experience was imprinted on his mind; he could not forget the scene. It occurred to Mahmud that even a seemingly insignificant amount of money to us can have a huge impact on people who live in less abundant circumstances than we do.

That got Mahmud thinking about all the young profession-als he knew who wanted to do something to make a positive difference but who seemed to have no clue how to do it because they had neither the money nor the power of wealthy philanthropists. Mahmud had a solution: an online clearinghouse for people to direct just a couple of hundred dollars a year to philanthropy.

In 2007 Mahmud and his wife, Nadia Khawaja, created the non-profit Jolkona Foundation (www.jolkona.org) to do just that. *Jolkona* is a Bengali word meaning "a drop of water." As Nadia explained it, "Small drops of money can add up and make a ripple of changing the world."

The couple funded the non-profit themselves, with help from volunteers and just one paid software developer. During the six-month test phase, Jolkona raised $3,000 from fifty friends. All donations go to charities, so they also created a separate place on the site where donations can be made to offset the organization's operating costs.

At Jolkona donors can pinpoint countries where they want to contribute and choose from five categories: cultural identity, education, empowerment, environment, and public health. Projects can be filtered by the amount of money needed—as little as five dollars—and the duration of donations can last anywhere from a few weeks to six years.

The foundation allows donors to channel funds to specific people and causes and allows them to monitor the impact their money is having. For example, the site offers "tangible proofs for every gift." That means if you grant fifty dollars for library books, you can find out exactly what books were bought with that money and which library and community received them. An individual's donations are broken down into charts and graphs that look something like a 401(k) portfolio. Mahmud calls these pages "resumes of good."

Mahmud's account shows an update on a project he's been supporting in India, helping a pregnant woman in a Calcutta slum. "Adopting" a mother and her baby costs $235, and donors can follow mom and baby's progress for three and a half years. For $40, schools for girls in Afghanistan can provide ten months of educational expenses. Donors can see the name of a girl, and at the end of ten months her benefactor can see her report card. And for just $30 you can buy seeds, tools, and training for women farmers in Sudan.

According to the couple, this is a very different model from what large, traditionally run charities do. In fact, it's almost impossible for small individual donors to find out exactly how their contributions are being used when they send a check to a "big box" charity. "It goes into this black hole," Mahmud told a reporter.

There is so much to love about this case study—anytime you hear someone (including yourself) say, "I don't have the resources to help other people," think about Mahmud, and what he did:

1. **Practiced conscious observation:** Mahmud was struck by something he saw on a trip home—he carried that idea with him and it bloomed into a business.

2. **Took action:** With help from his wife, Mahmud acted on the idea to start a charity despite the fact that he could have used any number of excuses not to—"I have no time," "I have no connections or influence," or "I have no money."

3. **Used skills he had while developing others:** Mahmud found a way around all three of those obstacles by using his computer skills to create a site that directs

small amounts of money to people who could use it in powerful ways.

4. **Started small, making financing doable:** Through the test phase, Mahmud garnered enough donations to demonstrate that Jolkona could be a viable charity and a model for other individuals to start philanthropic endeavors.

Perhaps most important, Jolkona is proof that one person making an observation is like a pebble thrown into a lake—the ripple effect can reach out to the edges.

Z2B EXERCISE: PRACTICE THE PRINCIPLES

It's time to live like a leader! Start living the fourteen principles on pages 233–34 today. How does it make you feel—which ones do you have the most trouble with? Note how it gets easier over time.

Z2B EXERCISE: READ ABOUT LEADERS

Learning about the people who have paved the way, made remarkable strides, invented stuff we love—it's just so uplifting. Each night before you go to bed, or in the morning when you wake up, read about an amazing person instead of listening to the depressing news or watching a rerun. Share the stories with your family—talk about them over dinner. The Internet is an embarrassment of riches in the leader department; it's very easy to find short biographies of interesting people. Start by plugging their names into your search engine—find out for yourself who these people are and what they did. Enjoy!

> Madam C. J. Walker
> Ruth Handler
> Scott Cook
> Anita Roddick
> Nelson Mandela
> Joan of Arc
> Rosa Parks
> Benjamin Franklin
> Booker T. Washington

Z2B EXERCISE: BE A MENTOR

The most immediate and direct way to be a leader and share your breakthroughs (and have more of your own) is to become a mentor to a young person. There are so many ways to be a mentor—most public schools have programs, as do organizations like the Y, churches, professional associations, and clubs like Rotary. Your company may even offer mentoring programs. I urge you to be a mentor for a year—in fact, I challenge you to do it. It will be an enriching experience, an instant feel-good jolt. It's your legacy we're talking about.

WET DOWN!

Hey, you made it to the end! In the Marines, when you're promoted to officer, you experience a ceremony called wetting down. It's not exactly formal—it used to involve tossing the new officer into the sea. A wetting-down celebration is hosted by the newly promoted officer at a local pub or bar. If the party is near a dock—well, be prepared to get tossed into the water. If not, get ready to be doused with water. A Marine would never waste liquor that way, because tradition says it's a valuable commodity in trading. Since I can't throw a bucket of water on you, I'm just going to say congratulations. You can have your own wet down at home. Remember, there's still more to do, but you're on the right footing. Take off from where you are, and good luck.

FLY- AWAYS

- Consider the legacy you are creating.

- Honor those whose shoulders you stand on by taking joy in your accomplishments.

- Wake up a leader—practice your leadership traits.

CHAPTER 8

Conclusion: Pass It On

I hope you come back to *Zero to Breakthrough* whenever you need a boost. You can dip in and out of the book and find just the right thing to remotivate. Remember that the process of breakthrough is not finite. You evolve, as do your breakthroughs. If you have children or know young people, please consider sharing the book with them. The old adage is true—they will inherit the earth.

I'm also interested in how you do with Zero to Breakthrough—I'd like to know your stories, both the triumphs and challenges. Share them with me at www.vernicearmour.com or clearedhot@vernicearmour.com.

In the meantime, here are a few final Fly-Aways to keep in mind:

- Recommit to your personal mission in life.

- Circle back, reference, and study the sections in the book you need the most.

- Create a master list of your breakthrough moments.

- Set clear and specific future goals.

- Commit to practicing discipline and excellent execution.

- Accept failures, account for them, and move on.

- Remember that you and you alone are the master of your own fate and future.

- Recognize that your potential is always expanding.

- Live your whole life with passion and purpose.

- Share the joy.

ACKNOWLEDGMENTS

This has been a long time coming. I remember standing outside the ready-room tent on the Syrian border. My flight crew was on alert, ready for another combat mission if we were called up. I was talking to my cousin Lucas Johnson, who'd already featured me in his book, *Finding the Good*. He had been seriously encouraging me to let him help document my story and write a book, but I wanted to actually *do* something first. I wanted there to be more than just a historic title. As I stood on the Syrian border talking to him on the duty satellite phone at two o'clock in the morning (during my second combat tour in Iraq), I told him I was ready. Thank you, Cuz. Thank you for taking me by the hand and leading me through this process. Without you, this book wouldn't exist, and I would have never met Linda Loewenthal, only the best literary agent in the world. Thank you, Linda, for your vision and belief in what this project could truly be.

I also want to thank the amazing group of professionals at Gotham Books: William Shinker, my publisher; Megan Newman, publisher and editor extraordinaire; and Miriam Rich, winner of the prestigious Most Patient Person in Publishing

Award (and one of the nicest, too). I am lucky to have such a world-class team behind my book and me. To Karen Kelly (KK), callsign "Double Duty," you were the best writing partner I could have asked for. You overdelivered every time and always exceeded my wildest expectations. Thank you for having my back; I'd go to battle with you any day!

"Baby, don't your lips get tired?" The famous words of my mom, Rean Jackson, crack me up every time I think about them. Of course, I was too young to remember it from my own recollection, but that's what you've always been good at . . . telling a fantastic story. Thank you for passing the gift of storytelling on to your only little "princess" among frogs. Even though I feel like I've given you all your gray hair, you've always been my biggest fan and just wanted me to be happy. I love you more . . .

He was Clarence Jackson to the world, and Dad to me: my favorite Marine. You are looking down on me from the blue skies above, and when I'm flying, I know you're right there next to me. You taught me that I had wings . . . tough wings that could take life's turbulence with humble courage. Thank you for teaching me to fight for what I wanted, no matter what.

My preparation for what went into this book started long before a tour of duty in Iraq. It actually started before I was even born. My great-grandmother, Rev. Dr. Falls, was one of the first African-American women ministers in the Unity church alongside Rev. Johnnie Colman. She would always say, "Something good has to come out of this." That mentality was passed down from my father, Gaston Armour, to me throughout my entire life. I call Dad "Mr. Philosophy": Whenever you ask a question, you'll get an answer and then some! Thank you,

Dad, for teaching me to be a deep thinker, a compassionate and loving member of everyone around me, and most of all for sharing the story of Uncle James . . . that we're all here for one purpose: to bless each other and help each other.

Gwen, you always kept it real and were always in my corner. Thank you for showing me (and Dad!) I didn't always have to take life so seriously!

There were many mentors along the way. Granny, Granddad, Grandmother and Grandfather Armour, I am standing on your amazing shoulders. Granny always said, "Anything worth having is worth working for!" I can only imagine what you went through and overcame that allowed me to accomplish what I have in life. Thank you for blazing the trail. My favorite teacher, Mrs. Williamson, I can still remember your smile and how you believed in me. Mr. Ryan let me play that trombone; thank you for giving me a chance.

When I had those tough times in the Corps, my senior leaders were right there ready to give guidance and keep me on the right path. To Misca, my battle-buddy, and Colonel Williams, thank you for keeping me sane through it all. To the Tuskegee Airmen and Lieutenant General Peterson (the Marine Corps' first black pilot and general), thank you for your shoulders. To Bessie Coleman and Amelia Earhart for blazing your amazing trails. To Dr. Mae Jemison, thank you for your mentorship and especially your friendship. To that black woman in the flight suit, whoever you are. I saw you during the hot summer of 1994 at Fort Bragg during Army ROTC Leadership Advanced Camp. I am your ripple . . . your legacy. Thank God you were in that tent that day; you changed my life.

To Dave Boufford and Les Brown, thank you for helping me achieve my dream of being a successful professional speaker. We're changing the world together and leaving a legacy.

There are soooo many other people I could thank. So, to my FlyGirls and FlyBoys (my FlyPeeps ... my support network), thank you for being there. To all my family and friends, thank you for loving me just the way I am.

Sometimes growing pains hurt. I am grateful for the growth, and there are no regrets. Every experience I have had has led me to this point and led me to develop what I now call a Breakthrough Mentality. It is with great gratitude that I continue to break through to new heights. I am honored and blessed to have had the opportunity to be of service.

Who needs a runway? Take off from where you are!

Vernice *"FlyGirl"* Armour

Break through your reality with a
Breakthrough Mentality™!

You are cleared hot.

INDEX

Note: Page numbers followed by a *t* refer to text boxes.